East African Odyssey

by

EMILEE HINES

Copyright © 2005 by Emilee Hines

First printing by Publish America, LLLP in 2005

Second printing by CreateSpace in 2013

First E-book published in 2012

All rights reserved except as permitted under the U. S. Copyright Act of 1976. No part of this publication may be reproduced, distributed, or transmitted in any form, or by any means, or stored in a database or retrieval system, without the prior written permission of the author.

Cover photograph by Rob Weaver.

Dedication

This memoir is dedicated to my fellow Teachers for East Africa, especially Ed Schmidt, who found us all again; to the Olivers; and to the memory of Margaret Lloyd.

Emilee Hines

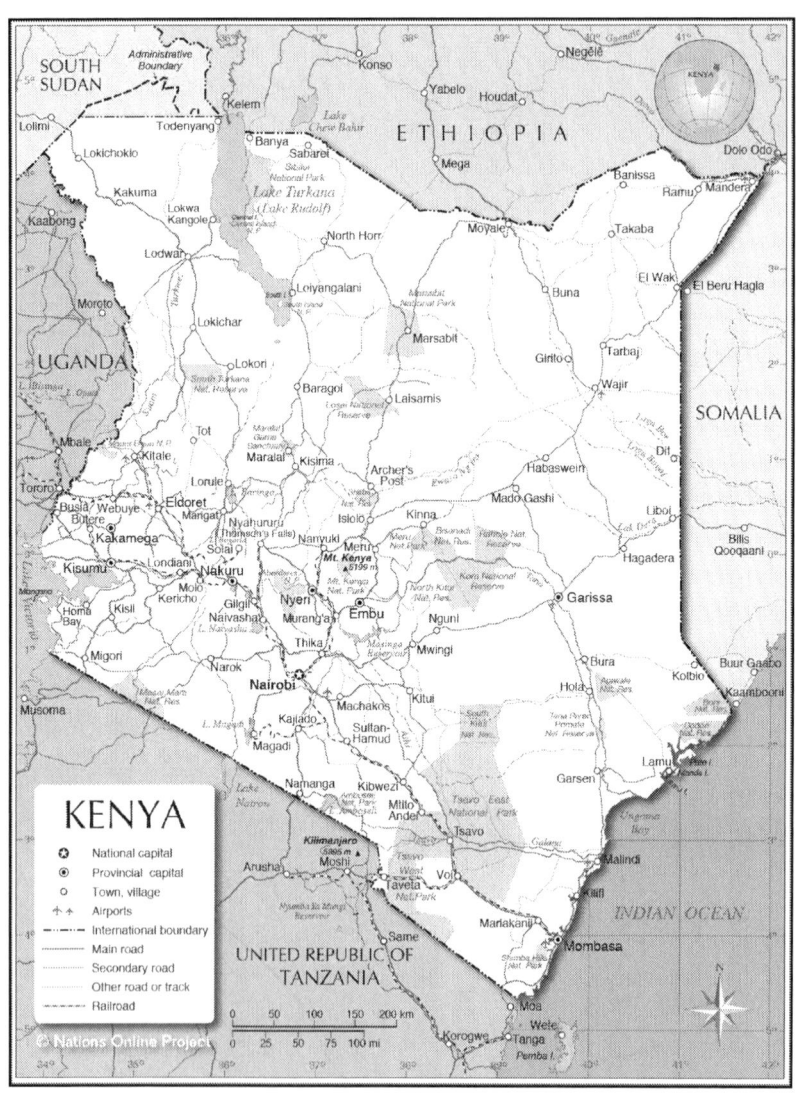

Map of Kenya

East African Odyssey

Contents

Dedication 3
Chapter 1: Going to Africa 3
Chapter 2: Kampala 7
Chapter 3: Surgit 14
Chapter 4: The Privileged Traveler 19
Chapter 5: Settling In 29
Chapter 6: Getting Out and Entertaining 38
Chapter 7: Romance 50
Chapter 8: The Floods 58
Chapter 9: Christmas in Kenya 69
Chapter 10: To the Frontier 78
Chapter 11: Changes 92
Chapter 12: Multiracial Kenya 101
Chapter 13: Duty and Decisions 110
Chapter 14: Easter Holidays 114
Chapter 15: Opportunities and Difficulties 120
Chapter 16: To Europe and Back 130
Chapter 17: Springtime 138
Chapter 18: Christmas II 147
Chapter 19: Uganda Again 152
Chapter 20: Faculty Friends and Rico 160
Chapter 21: Kilimanjaro, Malindi and the DEO 170
Chapter 22: Ray and Elections 177
Chapter 23: Leaving 193
AFTERWORD 203

Emilee Hines

Chapter 1: Going to Africa

I spent my first night in Kenya in the Nairobi Morgue, after riding four hundred miles in a pickup truck and being insulted in a hotel bar.

It wasn't what I'd expected when I applied for the Teachers for East Africa project, but Africa was full of surprises.

East Africa in 1961 was in the final days of British rule. The three races—Africans, Asians and Europeans—lived together in reasonable harmony and the promise of independence had not been tested. Animals flourished, seldom harmed by poachers. Trains and courts and the civil service worked, and jets could take us there and back.

It was exciting, frustrating and ultimately sad.

I was in graduate school that spring when I read about the joint Columbia University/U.S. Agency for International Development project to send teachers to Africa.

Africa! I had visions of grass huts, explorers hacking through steaming jungles, Hemingway hunting in the bush, Grace Kelly and Ava Gardner competing for Clark Gable. All the stereotypes. The photo accompanying the article had none of that. Instead, a room full of African students looked eagerly toward an unseen teacher, hungry for education. I could be that teacher, I thought, and applied for the project.

In April I was interviewed by Gordon Hagberg, one of the directors of the

U. S. Agency for International Development. I knew when his statements changed from 'if you go' to 'when you go' that I'd been chosen, and my notification telegram came ten days later. Africa seemed exciting beyond anything I'd ever done, but a little scary too.

A contract arrived spelling out the project conditions: we'd train at Columbia in New York and then at Makerere University in Kampala, Uganda. We might be assigned to schools in any of the four East African countries: Kenya, Tanganyika, Uganda or Zanzibar. We'd be paid what African teachers earned, plus a stipend from the U. S. Government. If we stayed for the two years' teaching, we'd receive a bonus and a plane ticket home. If not, no bonus, and we'd have to pay our own way home.

I got my first passport and shots to protect me from yellow fever, smallpox, typhoid, and typhus.

School ended. I had a few weeks at home with my parents to store up love and memories for my time away. When I visited the school where I'd taught, my former colleagues told me how 'brave' I was to go to go to Africa, a Southern woman who'd grown up in a segregated world. I didn't feel brave, just very lucky.

The weeks at Columbia flew by. We saw slides, heard lectures, and studied Swahili. Julius Nyerere, Prime Minister of Tanganyika, met with us, and the night before we left New York for Africa, we each received a copy of a well-wishing telegram from President Kennedy. It was all very heady.

We were divided into three groups. I was in A, experienced teachers. After five weeks at Makerere, we'd begin teaching. Group B, liberal arts majors, would spend nine months at Makerere studying British education and receive a master's degree before teaching. Group C, inexperienced education majors, studied at London and Makerere before being assigned a school. Our youngest two were just twenty, the oldest nearly forty. Men outnumbered women two to one.

On a July night, 102 of us in Groups A and B were bussed out to Idlewild Airport (now JFK) and boarded 'the plane from hell,' an old Constellation. Two of the four lavatories were blocked by luggage, and all the food brought aboard was breakfast. We were crammed in too tight for comfort, but we were too hyped up to sleep anyway. We were young and flexible. We'd endure anything to get to Africa, where we were sure adventure was waiting for us.

After breakfast and a refueling stop in the Azores, we headed for Kano, Nigeria. As we landed there at 2 a.m. Nigerian time, we blew a tire. A new one had to be flown from Portugal. We disembarked and sat watching lizards crawling on the white stucco walls of the airport in a steamy heat that the lazy ceiling fan couldn't dissipate.

Eventually daylight came, and we were fed breakfast again and put on a bus to see old Kano.

From a distance the town looked Biblical, like the Christmas card image of Bethlehem: low mud houses and an occasional date palm thrusting up from a flat sandy expanse. Up close, it was appalling. Goats wandered the dirt streets, and at the central watering hole in town, women washed clothes a few feet from where other women pushed aside green scum to dip water for home use and animals were drinking and defecating. Children followed us, begging for "*Baksheesh*," meaning alms, or trying to sell us fly-laden fried grasshoppers from shallow baskets balanced on their heads.

Our tire arrived and was installed, and we reboarded and took off for Entebbe, Uganda.

We landed at Entebbe at 2 a.m. Uganda time, thirteen hours past the time the project directors had planned a reception for us. There it all was, spread out on tables in the airport arrival lounge: tea cups, milk, sugar, limp cucumber and egg salad sandwiches, and little cakes whose frosting glistened with condensate.

We went through the motions, shaking hands with the few officials who had been summoned from their beds to greet us, and eating a token amount of the refreshments, which were by then anything but refreshing.

Groggy from lack of sleep, we boarded a bus from the Entebbe airport to Kampala. The streets were eerily quiet and dark, lit by pale blue or orangey-yellow lights.

At Makerere University we were issued sheets, towels and scratchy blankets, and sent to make up our beds.

 I struggled up the steps to my little room, unpacked a few things and fell asleep on a half-made bed about five a.m. I was in Africa, and I was cold.

Chapter 2: Kampala

I awoke to a different world.

The women's dorm at Makerere, Mary Stuart Hall, was cross-shaped, each wing only one room deep. My front door opened onto a long veranda and the rear onto a balcony with a view over the treetops to the city. Kano had been flat and dry, but Kampala was a city of hills, green with a riot of vegetation.

Down below, through fog, I could see patches of raw, red earth in between acacia trees blooming flame-orange. An African man pushed a bicycle up the steep hill toward the college.

After a bath in cold water and a breakfast of bread, jam and hot tea, we met the American Consul General and sleepily filled out papers. Besides registering as residents of East Africa, we indicated our preference for where and what subjects we'd like to teach. I chose Zanzibar and history, the worst possible choices for an American woman. I knew little of Zanzibar, only that it was exotic, and even less of East African history. Fortunately, the project directors chose a much better situation for me, though I didn't think so at first.

It poured rain that morning, but soon the sun came out and the steamy air cleared. It happened that way nearly every day. July is winter in the southern hemisphere, but the Equator passes through Uganda, so there's little seasonal change.

We had breakfast each morning at 7:30, tea break at ten, lunch at one, tea at 4:30 and dinner at eight. With what amounted to four or five meals a day, we were still hungry, partly because the food was so bland. Americans were outnumbered by Africans eight to one, and they liked the starchy diet of rice, potatoes, *matoke* (cooked green bananas) and cornmeal, served with a gravy of ground peanuts or chunks of meat.

We had a light class schedule, which left plenty of time to explore Kampala, a kaleidoscope of races, vehicles and architecture.

The third morning Joan and I we were waiting for the bus downtown when a car pulled up and the driver offered us a ride. He was English, and introduced himself as Mr. Gordette. We exchanged glances, decided there was safety in numbers, and accepted.

Mr. Gordette was a car salesman who thought he'd just spotted three likely American customers. As he drove, he told us about himself. "In the army in India until independence. Studied law, didn't like it. Spent time in Kenya putting down Mau Mau. Afterwards, I bought a coffee plantation. Sold it last year and moved here to Kampala."

He took us to his club for gin and lime drinks, then to lunch at La Quinta, a restaurant run by a Belgian countess who'd fled the Congo a year before.

Lunch was wonderful, and so different from Makerere fare. We began with creamy soup, moved on to steak and chips, mixed vegetables, and a smooth wine, all courtesy of Mr. Gordette. He lost interest somewhat when he learned that Joan and Pat would be students for nearly a year. I, on the other hand, would soon be teaching and might buy a car. He invited me out to dinner.

We had curry at dinner. After a few forkfuls I reached frantically for a drink. "Have you tried the green peppers?" he suggested, perhaps realizing by then that I wasn't going to buy a car from him. They were the African equivalent of jalapenos, and my mouth still burns in memory.

At a college dance, we American women were urged to dance with the other students, not just our TEA buddies. Some townspeople crashed the party too, adding to the male numbers. That's how Kay Hinklin met Surgit.

A few days later she came to my room and said, "Do me a favor and go out with Surgit. I'm supposed to have tea with him, but Dave's asked me to go riding on his motorcycle and I'd rather do that."

"Won't Surgit mind the switch?" I asked.

"No, he just wants to go out with an American. He'll be here in a few minutes. He's a good-looking Indian with a red car. Just tell him you're taking my place."

Strange as it sounds, I agreed. She'd barely left when I heard a car roaring up the hill. It came to a stop just below our veranda, and a man got out, a man so handsome he almost took my breath away. He was tall and slim, and had black curly hair and a moustache. He looked up and smiled, a flash of white teeth against his tawny skin.

Two of the Indian girls who lived in Mary Stuart came by and spoke to him, then walked on, muttering.

When I raced down to introduce myself, he was laughing. "What's so funny?" I asked.

"Those girls. They said, 'Poor Surgit. He's no proper Sikh anymore. He's cut his hair, shaved his beard, thrown away his turban, and now he's going out with an American.' They think I'm evil."

But he wasn't. He was kind and attentive and courtly, and treated me like a princess. And he didn't mind that I was a substitute. We drove to Lake Victoria Hotel at Entebbe and had tea on the lawn, looking out to the lake. Water lapped softly against the sand, and the air was scented with frangipani. A crested crane strolled by, its multicolored tail spread iridescent in the sunlight. It was exotic and magical. We walked in the cool shaded paths of the hotel garden and talked. With my Southern accent and his Indian one, I wondered later just how much we actually communicated that afternoon. Well enough anyway that he invited me to La Quinta for dinner and dancing.

La Quinta's African band copied hit tunes. Late in the evening the band leader came around to the tables with a mike, asking us to sing a few lines of "Banana Boat Song." I did, and the next thing I knew, they were urging me to come up on the stage and sing with the band. Every time I went to La Quinta for the next three weeks, I was invited up to sing. One night I protested, "I don't know the words to 'Waltzing Matilda.'" A man from the audience called out, "Sing anyway, lassie."

Surgit took me for curry and samosas, for chateaubriand and meringue Chantilly: wonderful, tasty food. We drove at night when the moon was shrouded with clouds risen from Lake Victoria and stopped by Namirembe Cathedral to look down on Kampala. He told me about himself: that he'd studied in Germany to repair Mercedes cars, and now managed the dealership in Kampala. He brought me flowers from his garden, and I put them in a paper cup. On our next date he brought flowers in a brass vase. He made no demands on me other than being with him and having a good time.

At lunch one day I mentioned that Surgit let me drive his little car. Another teacher burst out laughing. "A little car? Little! It's an Aston Martin."

"Is that special?"

"It probably cost ten times what we'll make teaching a year."

It wasn't quite as much fun driving the car after that.

I worried that I might harm it. Besides, it had manual transmission.

The next week all of Group A went to observe in local African schools. I was assigned to Trinity College, a Catholic girls' secondary school near Kampala.

In mid-week I went with one of the teachers and a group of students on a field trip to Jinja that covered all the bases of Uganda's commerce.

We toured Owen Falls Dam that harnessed the force of Lake Victoria as it pours northward, forming the mighty Nile. Ancient Egyptians sacrificed to the river god Osiris to bring on the annual flooding, which was actually caused by heavy rainfall in Uganda.

The dam furnished electric power for much of Kenya as well as for the local sugar refinery, textile mill and copper smelter. In all three factories, raw material came in—sugar cane, bales of cotton and ore—and emerged as finished products: bags of brown granular sugar, bolts of bright cloth and copper ingots.

We passed African *shambas*, sturdy mud and wattle houses surrounded by banana plants, gardens and flamboyant flowers.

Near Jinja I saw my first tea plantation, delicate dark green shrubs shaded by tall eucalyptus trees. The spicy, biting fragrance of eucalyptus ever after has evoked memories of Uganda. Eucalyptus and some pungent hedges also surrounded Trinity, and graced the grounds of the Imperial Hotel in Kampala, where we Americans sometimes escaped for an indulgent afternoon tea.

The Mother Superior came from England to inspect Trinity that week. This entailed a welcoming ceremony, with cake and sweetened milky tea, followed by student speeches.

The Trinity teachers told of a disruptive visit to the school by the Kabaka, king of Uganda. After having the girls parade past him, he pointed out one and ordered her brought to the palace to be one of his wives.

The faculty were horrified and frightened. They couldn't defy the king, but they were supposed to protect their students. With great trepidation, they sent for the parents, telling them to come immediately. The parents arrived, fearing that their daughter had succumbed to malaria, sleeping sickness or an accident.

When the principal revealed what had happened, smiles creased the parents' faces, and the father exclaimed, "God be praised! The Lion has roared again in Uganda." Their daughter would be pampered and provided for financially, and through her, so would they.

I was getting to know Kampala: the layout of the streets, the hours of shopping, the art of bargaining, and what shops sold what. Kampala was a hilly, crowded, vibrant city, its streets teeming with black and brown people. It had been the capital of the ancient Baganda kingdom and thus became the country's capital, though it is no more centrally located than Washington, D. C. is to the United States. The airport was located at Entebbe, on Lake Victoria, because the first air service into East Africa was by flying boats that landed on the lake.

Stately black Baganda women wearing voluminous long dresses carried heavy loads balanced on their heads. Men walked ahead or rode bicycles. Indian women in brilliant saris, with colorful spots painted onto their faces, strolled or rode in cars. Throughout the crowd were Indian men in dark suits and white turbans.

Sometimes, after spending several hours in Kampala surrounded by dark-skinned people, I'd catch a glimpse of myself reflected in a shop window and think, "Who is that pale person?" Or I'd glance down at my own light-skinned hand in surprise. This was a dark world, and I was the alien.

One night I went with Surgit to a boxing match between the champions of England and of Uganda. Because of the altitude—Kampala was some 3500 feet above sea level—the Africans won easily. Long before the ninth round, the English boxers were panting for breath and falling back against the ropes. They'd arrived only that morning after an overnight flight, and hadn't had a chance to get acclimated to the altitude or the humidity.

The Ugandan former heavyweight champion, older than the other boxers and built like a bear, fought that night. He hammered away at his white-skinned opponent, connecting relentlessly with bruising blows. Within minutes the loser was sagging and punchy.

"Who is that boxer?" I asked Surgit.

"Idi Amin," he said.

The ruthless boxer was later to become the ruthless dictator of the country.

Chapter 3: Surgit

The next weekend Surgit invited me to visit his friends in Masindi, a town in northwestern Uganda across Lake Albert from the Congo. I had no idea what to expect, but I wanted to see as much of Africa as I could and I liked Surgit, so I said yes. Were the people we were visiting Indians? "They're Europeans," he told me, before I could ask. 'European' meant Caucasian, or light-skinned people, from anywhere, not just Europe.

As we left Kampala and paved roads behind, houses became farther apart, and after a while we passed hillsides of banana plants, coffee plantations where the trees held white blossoms and red coffee berries at the same time, and papyrus swamps. The tall papyrus reeds, used long ago to make paper, spread across the marshes, their tops feathered with tiny blossoms.

The road was red earth, and after a sudden downpour, it became a sticky goo. The car slid perilously if Surgit turned the wheel too quickly, so we slowed.

As he drove, Surgit told me about the Stonemans. "Jan is a snake expert, and her husband is a fisheries officer," he said. "I met Jan when she came in to buy a Mercedes."

We stopped for tea at an old railroad hotel, so it was almost dark when we arrived. Jan's husband was recovering from bilharzia, a water-borne ailment that produced liver flukes, and had already gone to bed. There were other guests, including a young man whose name, Nigel, I finally had Jan spell for me. Because of Jan's accent, I thought she said My-jo. I never asked what she made of my accent.

I had a room of my own, and the next morning I was awakened by a tap on the door. "Jambo, Memsahib," an African servant greeted me, a phrase I was to hear many times over the next two years. He held a tray of tea: an individual teapot, a tiny pot of hot milk with a strainer to remove the milk skim, a cup and saucer and a plate of sugar cookies, called biscuits.

"Jambo. Asante sana," I said, thanking him as I took the tray inside. I didn't hear anybody else stirring, but after I finished tea I dressed and crept out, eager to see this exciting world.

Jan was in the lounge having her tea. She showed me a small room where she had tubs of frogs, turtles, and snakes, and three batches of baby crocodiles, each about a foot long. When she poked at them, they hissed ferociously and snapped their jaws, practicing for adulthood when they'd devour other animals or unwary humans who wandered too close to the water.

Outside, Jan had full-grown crocodiles in cages, and a wart hog named Tweedle tethered to a post. Three huge dogs guarded everything, and a python, Peter, had a small room of his own. Several glass aquariums held snakes, which she was raising for venom.

"If we don't like a guest, we put Peter or one of the snakes in their closet," she said with a grin.

"If I didn't see Peter this morning, does it mean you like me, or should I just be extra careful each time when I open the closet door?" I asked.

She just grinned.

After Surgit and the rest of the group had breakfast, we piled into two cars and set out across the grassy plains for Murchison Falls. We forded small streams, following tracks through the tall grass. Suddenly we came to a stop. A herd of elephants crossed the road ahead of us. What a thrill! They were like big gray mountains, moving at their own pace, unafraid of cars, secure as lords of their world. Years later I wept unashamedly when I heard that Idi Amin's troops had slaughtered hundreds of thousands of these gentle giants.

At Murchison Falls the water of Lake Albert joins the Victoria Nile to form the White Nile. It then flows northward through Ethiopia, picking up more water from the Blue Nile at Khartoum. This was its source. The great river crashed through a 20-foot chasm, throwing spray high into the air and creating a roar we could hear long before we saw the falls. We crossed a wooden footbridge, picked our way across rocks above the falls and sat down finally to our picnic lunch, at three o'clock.

The next day we drove westward to Butiaba, on Lake Albert, and passed a rubber plantation, the first I'd seen. Straight-trunked trees with big shiny leaves lined both sides of the road, so dense we were almost in darkness.

At the lake we took one of the Stonemans' three motorboats out to an island. The men fished. I tried fly-casting too, but caught only an occasional tree limb.

Lunch was primitive. The Stonemans' cook had forgotten to pack utensils or cups, so we tore off chunks of bread and dug corned beef out of cans with our hands. We peeled and ate hard-boiled eggs, wedges of Gruyere cheese and sweet, finger-sized bananas. We even managed to eat canned peaches with our fingers, the juice running down our arms to drip off our elbows. Afterward, we rinsed the cans and drank tea from them.

Before the day was out we saw hundreds more elephants. This, I thought, was really Africa.

On the way back to Kampala that night Surgit and I met only six cars in over one hundred thirty miles, and passed through three villages, no towns. In every village dilapidated little shops bore signs for Pepsi, Coke, Johnson's Baby Powder, and Kodak. American business had been there ahead of us.

A few days later we were told our teaching assignments. When I found I wasn't going to Zanzibar but to Kenya, I was crushed. I told myself I'd hate Kenya, and might go home by Christmas. Fortunately I didn't say that to the interviewer.

"You've got one of the best assignments," he said. "Your school is about 40 miles from Nairobi, on a paved road, and the classrooms and housing are only three years old. You'll be teaching girls and young women—and a few older than you are, who are coming back for refresher courses—to be primary teachers. However, your principal expects most of the students to marry within a year of completing the course; an education adds to their bride price. So you'll need to prepare them to be good wives s well as teachers."

What did I know about being a good African wife?

Meanwhile, life improved at Makerere. Some Americans organized morning tea. For a shilling each—about 14 cents—we could share bread, cheese, fruit and instant coffee.

Swahili was beginning to make sense too. When the Stonemans came to Kampala, Surgit entertained them, and I helped. I asked his houseboy in Swahili for a knife to cut the sandwiches and got it! Sometimes I could even understand a joke in Swahili.

I had letters from home telling how hot and dry it was, that tobacco was ready for harvest and watermelons were ripe. In Kampala we were grateful that it hadn't rained for three days. But it was cold. While we were close to the Equator, my most-worn garment was a heavy wool sweater.

In late August all of East Africa celebrated Jomo Kenyatta's release from imprisonment on the Northern Frontier of Kenya. He'd been interned for seven years for Mau Mau activities, and was the most likely candidate for President of Kenya after its independence.

Makerere held a celebratory party in Main Hall to end all parties. The floor throbbed from pounding footsteps as we danced to the African band. African students wore their tribal costumes and waved *dashikis*, a kind of leather flywhisk, as they shouted "Kenyatta na Uhuru!" I'm not a beer drinker, but my American colleagues more than made up for what I didn't drink. Tusker Lager was the favorite brand among the Europeans, and a few sampled *pombe*, made from fermented bananas, the favorite of the African students.

Class attendance was skimpy the next day. Some were sick from pombe and many had headaches, but few complained. We'd had an authentic African experience.

Surgit

Chapter 4: The Privileged Traveler

Surgit offered to take me to my new job in Kenya.

"That's a long way and a lot of trouble for you," I objected. "And the project will give me a train ticket."

"I've been intending to go to Kenya anyway," he said. "I have friends and family in Nairobi."

I accepted. I wondered if we'd go in the Aston Martin or his Mercedes. As it turned out, neither. He showed up in a Chevrolet pickup, along with another Asian man going to visit his brother who was chief surgeon at the hospital in Machakos. We loaded my belongings and set off on our four hundred mile journey.

We crossed the Nile at Jinja, stopping briefly to get me an international driving license.

About a hundred miles from Kampala we entered a land of sparse vegetation, where vultures squatted in scrub trees and baboons hid in elephant grass beside the highway. About that time the pavement ran out.

For the next two hundred miles we bounced along on a dirt road, or murram, as the surface was called. The highway department graded the existing roads and spread a layer of gravel and clay, which soon migrated to the sides.

We climbed steadily, and the air grew cooler and drier. We crossed into Kenya, and it began to rain, great pelting drops that made mud on the dirty windshield and turned the road into a bog.

In the midst of the rain we stopped for three nuns. They scrambled into the back of the pickup and huddled under the tarp to keep dry. Soon after it stopped raining, we picked up a male African hitchhiker. With few vehicles, people in East Africa trusted in the kindness of drivers, and drivers trusted the honesty of the hitchhikers. In Eldoret, the highest town on the Kenya-Uganda highway, we dropped off all our riders.

The Kenya Highlands are one of the most beautiful areas on earth. I felt as if we were driving across the very rim of the world, with an immense sky all around us. Occasionally across a vast field I could see a farmhouse and its cluster of outbuildings. The earth was dark and fertile looking, and a hint of wood smoke hung in the air. When I sniffed and commented, Surgit said the Africans made charcoal from the eucalyptus trees.

We passed Lake Nakuru, pink with the last light of sunset and with flamingos taking wing off the lake. We wound our way along the road built by Italian prisoners of war up the Escarpment to a point that overlooked Nairobi. The moon had risen, and the air was chilly. Nairobi glowed like a jeweled carpet in the distance. Surgit pulled over to let me look, and his friend asked quietly, "What do you think of Kenya now?"

I loved it then, but in the next hour I was to dislike it, or at least one aspect of it. Surgit dropped his friend off and parked on Delamere Avenue in Nairobi. He opened the door to a small bar and said, "You can wait for me here. I need to find a phone and call my cousin Mohan." He ordered me a drink, dropped his packet of cigarettes on the bar and left.

A beefy, red-faced man came in, climbed up on a bar stool two spaces from me and asked for a cigarette.

I pushed Surgit's pack across to him and said, "They're my friend's, but I'm sure he won't mind."

He said, "Oh, you're American."

"Yes," I said.

"Why don't you Americans go home? Don't you think you've caused enough trouble in the world?"

I was too shocked to think of a reply, and for once I held my tongue.

About that time Surgit came back in and said, "Mohan has a houseful of guests, but my friend Manny says we can stay with him and his wife."

The man at the bar shoved the cigarettes back toward me. "Are you with him? You silly slut."

I had to grab Surgit's arm to keep him from hitting the man, though I wanted to myself. In two sentences he'd insulted both of us.

Back in the pickup, I said, "How can I live here if they're all like that?"

"They're not," Surgit said. "He's drunk."

I had calmed down somewhat by the time Surgit pulled up in front of a building labeled 'morgue.' "What are we doing here?" I asked.

"Manny manages the morgue. He and his wife live in a flat attached to the morgue. He has to be available at all hours."

Manny and his wife, Indians like Surgit, were gracious hosts, though the conversation at dinner was unusual as Manny told gruesome stories of massacred bodies and fascinating stories about Congolese gold being smuggled out in false-bottom coffins. (I later used one of these stories to write an adventure novel, *Coffins from the Congo*.) We had dinner and coffee, and by bedtime I'd gotten over my squeamishness about bodies lying just down the hall past a metal door.

The next morning we drove out to Machakos Teachers College, a low-lying group of pink-roofed cement buildings set in among rolling hills. Miss Anderson, the teacher on duty, welcomed me, showed me which flat was to be mine, and unlocked it so Surgit could move my things in. Then she served tea, all the while with a slightly puzzled expression. Surgit was probably the first Indian man who'd had tea in her flat. I'd started my tenure at Machakos on the 'wrong foot,' by arriving with an Asian.

That afternoon Surgit and Mohan took his sister's children and me to Karen, a country club in the former home of Karen Blixen, who wrote *Out of Africa* as Isak Dinesen. Surgit rented horses and we all rode, then sat on the veranda and had drinks. I hadn't read *Out of Africa*, and didn't appreciate the significance of where we were. I only enjoyed the view of the Ngong Hills, and being with Surgit and Mohan. Mohan was almost as handsome as Surgit, but stockier and without a moustache.

The next day we went to Fifteen Falls, north of Nairobi, for a picnic of prawn curry, crispy thin papadums, and *samosas*, fried pastries filled with spicy meat.

"This is where part of the film 'Mogambo' was made," Mohan said. "Surgit and I both met Clark Gable."

Surgit nodded. "We all laughed like crazy when Clark Gable stepped through that bit of bamboo there and said this looked like gorilla country. There's not a gorilla in five hundred miles of here."

I said I'd like to visit Zanzibar before the school term started, ten days away. "You can visit the tea plantation in Tanganyika, too," Surgit said, as casually as if everybody owned one. "Then you can drive with Mohan's brother to Dar es Salaam, fly to Zanzibar from there, fly to Mombasa and catch the train back up-country."

It sounded complicated, with a lot of spots where something could go wrong, but it sounded exciting, and I accepted.

On Monday morning Surgit left for Kampala after helping me buy plane and train tickets. That night Mohan took me to the train, handing me a new British magazine and a bouquet of flowers for my journey. I shared a compartment with an English woman and had dinner on the train, complete with champagne, for ten shillings, then about $1.40.

The next morning the train stopped at a bleak, uninhabited spot. We were supposed to get into Mombasa at eight, and I'd take a van from the city to the airport. As seven, then seven-thirty, came and went with no movement, I began to panic.

Finally a conductor came through telling us the problem: the train ahead of us had hit a rhino and derailed, blocking the tracks. We'd be bussed into Mombasa.

I had to make that plane. Surgit had called Bill, who would be meeting me, and there was only one flight to Tanga that day. If I went all the way into Mombasa, I'd never get to the airport on time. I persuaded the bus driver to put me and my suitcase out at the road to the airport.

The bus pulled off and there I stood, a lone woman in a strange place. It was miles from the main road to the airport. I started walking, stalking along as fast as I could in high heels and a silk suit, carrying my full suitcase, and sweating in the morning humidity.

I'd only gone a half-mile or so when a Jeep pulled up beside me. I turned, willing to ride with whoever it was. The driver said, "So, Emilee, you're determined to go to Zanzibar, I see. Get in." It was one of the administrators of the TEA project. He got me to the airport on time. He was going to Zanzibar.

Bilbander Gill, Mohan's brother, had no trouble recognizing me, as I was the only woman to get off the plane, but he had some trouble getting me through customs and immigration. I was so unsophisticated that I didn't know not to put my passport in my suitcase. Eventually the officials allowed me to collect my suitcase, open it and show them my passport. I never put it in a suitcase again.

Bill was only 21, but he managed the family's 3,700-acre tea plantation, tea processing plant and lumbering operations, called Sikh Saw Mills, that employed 600 people. I waited in his office until four, when a British couple and their two sons arrived and we all drove to the plantation.

The estate covered the tops of three mountains about twenty-five miles outside Tanga, and was like a little kingdom. The house had four bedrooms, its own dynamo for electricity, and a wireless system that connected it with the office in town.

Billbander Gill, center, with guests

The next morning Bill drove us into the rain forest where monkeys swung through the trees, and we toured the tea processing plant. I'd imagined the tea leaves picked, dried and sent away to be encased in little bags. Instead, the buds and tiny leaves were crushed, mixed with water and fermented for several days. The mixture was spread on wire screens to dry in big ovens and sorted by size and color into foil-lined wooden boxes. The Gills' tea, carrying the label Bulwa Estates, was prized at tea auctions, where most of it sold to Brooke Bond.

"Every visitor gets a box of tea as a souvenir," Bill announced.

Each box was about a foot in each direction, and I couldn't imagine how I'd get it on the plane and take it back to Machakos with me. Bill saw my problem. "We'll have one waiting for you in Nairobi," he said.

"Can you send it to my family instead?"

He got my parents' address.

After two days at the tea plantation Bill and I set off for Dar es Salaam, 210 miles away, in his Mercedes convertible. About a hundred miles of the route was paved, out of Tanga and into Dar. The stretch between was a dusty track across the desert. Even though it was springtime in East Africa, the three-year drought had stressed the trees. Their leaves were red and yellow, like autumn back home. Blue morning glories bloomed along the way, and monkeys played in the trees. We had to stop once to let a dozen monkeys cross, each carrying ears of corn they'd stolen from some farmer's field.

The few cars we met drove in our dust, and we in theirs. By the time we reached Dar es Salaam, everything about me was the same color, dusty tan. Muddy streaks trickled down the back of my bare legs where I'd sweated.

Dar was lovely, its crowded streets bordered by palm trees and pastel stone houses with windows open to the sea air. The week there was like being in a movie. While Bill visited friends and attended a tea planters' convention, he arranged for me to stay with a Goan couple who worked for the Gill empire.

The first party, in honor of Mrs. Indira Gandhi, was held at the headquarters of the Tanganyika African National Union, a grand new building. A valet opened the door for us and drove the car away. I took Bill's arm and we mounted the steps in the glare of brilliant spotlights and the occasional flash of a camera. I felt like a celebrity, though the crowd was really there hoping to see Mrs. Gandhi or Julius Nyerere, Prime Minister of the country. I was glad I'd packed my black cocktail dress.

That evening I was introduced to Dr. Nyerere and Mrs. Gandhi, and I tried to make suitable remarks. Everyone there was either high up in Tanganyika government or very rich—except me. Then like Cinderella, I was taken back to my tiny room.

A sundowner the next evening was on the lawn at the home of friends of Bill's. The American consul and his wife were there, as well as high-ranking officials from the governments of Tanganyika and Nyasaland. And the food was wonderful: samosas, asparagus rolls, cashews, lamb kabobs and shrimp.

During the day I went to the empty beach along the Indian Ocean. On the way there with Bill and his friends one day I got a lesson in cultural differences. As we stopped for a light, several Indian girls in saris were shepherded by a chaperone across the street ahead of us. The men ogled the plumpest one, admiring the way she swayed as she walked, and staring at the four inches of bare midriff between her blouse and skirt. Those few inches of flesh were sexier to them than my legs, bare from the knee down. The same group was in the water near where we swam later that day, and the men kept swimming close, only to have the chaperone come between them and the girls, whose silk saris clung wetly to their bodies.

From Dar I flew to Zanzibar, as exotic as I'd expected, but small. Bill had called ahead and a lovely woman, the wife of a friend, came to my hotel and took me driving around the island, and to tea at her house.

Dinner at the hotel was dreary and bland after the wonderful seafood and curries of Dar, and my mosquito-netted bed was lumpy and uncomfortable.

The next morning I wandered around old town Zanzibar by myself, admiring the elaborately carved Arabic doors, sampling red bananas, sipping the delicious liquid from a green coconut and sitting on a stone wall watching dark-sailed dhows gliding into the harbor. Zanzibar even smelled exotic: a mixture of curry, fruit, salt air and cloves—which flourished on the island.

I had a strange feeling in Zanzibar that I've never had anywhere else, that I had been there before. As I approached a cross street, I knew just what lay around the corner, and I was right. The doors, the buildings, were exactly as I'd seen them in my mind. It was that strange attraction that had prompted me to list Zanzibar as my choice for a teaching post.

Later, as the plane took off to cross the stretch of water from Zanzibar to Mombasa, I looked down as long as I could see the island, the palm trees and the ocean. It was beautiful, but small and confining and Arabic. And I had fallen in love with the Kenya Highlands. I was glad I'd seen Zanzibar, but satisfied to leave it. My destiny waited in Kenya, though I didn't know it at the time.

The next morning as the train climbed up-country from Mombasa, we rumbled past miles of baked desert marked by thorn trees and baobabs, and sometimes the cone of an extinct volcano. Presently a group of mud-colored buildings appeared, and the train came to a stop at Athi River. My principal, Miss Alison Shrubsole, was waiting there to drive me to Machakos, twenty-five miles away.

As we turned off the main highway onto the Machakos road, Miss Shrubsole pointed to the hills ahead of us. "Those are the Muwa Hills that Hemingway described in his *Green Hills of Africa*."

They didn't look green to me. Nothing did. My lips were parched from the dry air and the earth was cracked. "Is it always this dry here?"

"No. We're in the third year of drought, and we're hoping desperately for rains within a month. So many people and animals are starving."

She turned onto the murrum road that led to the college, and my holiday ended.

Chapter 5: Settling In

Holidays were over. I could unpack, get to know my colleagues and the college, and do what I had come to do—teach young African women.

When term began September 13, I was given my schedule, a strange one indeed. I was to teach 21 class periods each week in English, African and British history, and Domestic Science, as the British called home economics. I'd hated home ec. in high school and I'd never taken any college courses in it, but in Africa faculty pitched in to cover classes for whoever was on leave. The domestic science teacher was on leave, and it was my turn to take her classes.

Three mornings a week I began teaching at 7:30, and on Mondays I had class until 4:30 in the afternoon. Wednesday afternoons were free for everybody, but we had classes on Saturday morning. I copied my schedule into a notebook and taped the original onto the door of my tiny refrigerator to make sure I went to the right class at the right time.

When I stood in assembly to be introduced to the students and stared out at the roomful of faces, I was dismayed. How could I ever tell them apart? They didn't really look alike, but there didn't seem to be enough difference for me to connect names and faces. I was used to classes of both girls and boys; some blondes, brunettes and redheads, all dressed differently. Though they came from many different tribes, the African girls were almost all the same shade of brown, and they were all wearing their pink physical education uniforms.

This helpless feeling often happens when anyone meets large numbers of a different race. Indeed, the girls later told me they couldn't tell one lecturer from another at first either, even though we ranged in age from 25 to 60, had varying hair colors, and our weights went from 120 to nearly 200!

When I met my first class that afternoon the students were wearing different colored dresses, which made it easier to differentiate them, but when I looked at my class roll, I couldn't pronounce their names.

Bravely I worked my way down the list, from Ayugi to Waichanguru and Wanjiri. Most names weren't as difficult as I'd first thought, but some of my pronunciations brought a snicker from the class, and the rather sullen explanation from the owner of the mispronounced name, "It is said—"

To make matters worse, some of the students told me both names on my roll were correct, but they were called by yet another name, which I wrote in the margin as phonetically as I could from the girl's pronunciation.

I spent the first days in a fog. I didn't know the names of things, where they were kept, or the procedure to go through to get anything done. All the government agencies and people seemed to go under a set of initials, like PEO, DEO, DC, and PWD, which my British colleagues were all familiar with and used easily. I arrived late at one faculty meeting or didn't show up at all for another. I couldn't make sense out of the sheaf of papers announcing various things I must attend and attend to.

In addition, we all had duties. My second day of teaching I was assigned to check that the students cleaned up the dining hall after supper, and at ten I had to walk around to all the dorms and cottages to make certain lights were out and the girls were quiet. Another teacher went with me that first time, but after that, I was on my own.

Because of my American accent, the principal assigned me to teach grammar and literature only. An honors graduate from England taught speech, trying valiantly to wipe out the African quirk of transposing *l* and *r*, so that 'lorry,' their word for a truck, came out 'rolly.' 'Liver' and 'river' were interchanged.

The girls were excellent students. They would stand when I entered class, wait for me to say, "Good morning, class," and respond in courteous unison, "Good morning, Miss Hines." It came out 'Mees Inz.' Only when I asked them to be seated would they sit down.

They spoke English in addition to their own tribal language and often Swahili as well and made a conscious effort to expand their vocabularies. They were eager to learn, and paid such close attention to me and to everything I said that it was almost unnerving. They carried little vocabulary notebooks, and when I used a word they weren't familiar with, hands would go up and someone would ask, "Please, Miss, how is that word spelled?" I'd write it on the chalkboard and someone else would ask, "Is it a verb? Can it be a noun? Can it have another meaning?" We often spent a quarter of the class on vocabulary, and I loved it. Every teacher wants to see that her students have actually learned what she's taught. At Machakos, I did see.

The students' homework was neatly done and turned in on time. Occasionally they made grammar mistakes, but so did most people. Besides awkward verb tenses, they came up with some unusual word usages. One in particular I thought was apt. Instead of writing, "I had no alternative," my student wrote, "As I had no otherwise." I liked that expression. Often I too had no 'otherwise' to some situation I'd have liked to avoid.

In history I read frantically about explorers, chieftains and British monarchs, trying to learn more than my students knew, and in domestic science I set up demonstrations of laundry and cleaning. I soon realized that they already knew perfectly good methods for doing most household chores. I could help them learn to use electrical appliances, for they used them at college and would want them eventually for their own homes. Maybe this, I thought, was what the interviewer had meant when he'd said my principal wanted us to prepare the girls to be good wives.

"Miss Hines, why don't European women get married?" my students asked.

"They do," I said.

"Not here," was the answer.

Based on their observation of European women in Kenya, it was accurate. Their lecturers were almost all single women.

"Most Europeans who marry stay home and have families," I said. "Only a few choose to come to Africa and teach far from home. And most of us will go back and marry."

I showed them photos of my family. The one of my parents standing in front of their brick home especially interested them. "He has only the one wife?" one student asked doubtfully. When I said that was true for most Americans, some pitied my parents. My father must be poor to only have one wife, and she would have much work to do, without younger wives to help out.

Several girls said they wanted to be their husband's only wife. They intended to live in town, have a job, and never need a second wife to help with farm work.

"But they are so young to have a child as big as you," another mirated. Actually, my parents had been in their thirties when I was born, ancient for Africans, but they had aged well. My mother, in particular, looked better than an African woman her age would look—if an overworked African woman even reached her late fifties.

They had no photos of their families, for they had no cameras, and might have been embarrassed to show photos of their homes.

My students were courteous and pleasant, but we were never to become friends. They were at college to learn how to be teachers, not to be buddies with their lecturers. The British system was structured and there was always a barrier between lecturers and students. I'd learned as a very young teacher that getting too friendly with students could lead to ineffectiveness and discipline problems, so in Africa I accepted the system and didn't push to change it.

American schools begin in August or September, but the East African school year began in January with a three month term, then a month's vacation, repeated three times. We were in the final term, and I was expected to give exams within six weeks on material I had never taught!

I borrowed student notes and with the help of other teachers made out exams. No multiple choice or True-False. These girls had to write a suitable essay on each topic.

Moreover, those who were soon to graduate must do student teaching.

The college was new and thriving. It had been built by the British partially as a thank-you to the Wakamba tribe for not joining Mau Mau during The Emergency in the 1950s. MTC, as it was abbreviated, had opened in mid-1958.

The college was in sight of the tarmac (paved) road leading to Machakos town, and just opposite where the murram road to the college turned off was a Hindu crematorium. We sometimes saw flower-encircled bodies being burned there and heard the chants of mourners.

The campus was horseshoe-shaped. Along the outer perimeter were servants' quarters, then staff quarters—where gardeners, the office clerk and night watchmen lived with their families. Next came the principal's house, eight faculty duplexes, a row of sheds for parking faculty cars, and finally a cluster of cottages where students took turns living.

Inside the horseshoe, and divided from the outside by the driveway, the dining hall at one end faced offices and storerooms at the other. Dorms flanked the dining hall; farther on, next to the office, were two long strips of classrooms.

All around our campus was pasture, in September 1961 parched and cracked from a three-year drought. Here and there small acacias, or thorn trees, clung to life. To one side across the pasture was the boys' secondary school and straight ahead lay the country club. I could climb a stile, cross the pasture and golf club, and reach town in a few minutes.

My Flat at Machakos Teachers College

I had half of the fourth duplex. The religious education teacher had the other half, and at quiet times I could hear sermons on her radio. We could also hear each other flush the toilet or run a bath. However, there were very few quiet times. House servants worked with the kitchen doors open, and called out to one another or sang discordant little tunes. Students were free to come to our flats at any time for help, local merchants made deliveries, and peddlers showed up at lunchtime with carvings, baskets, paintings and fruit to sell. Machakos Training College was lively.

The back of our flats faced the road, so that visitors had to walk around the house to reach the front door. Most people came and went through the kitchen. Someone would approach the open door, tap and call out, "*Hodi*?" I'd answer, "*Kuja*," inviting them in.

The kitchen had an electric stove, a sink, a big wooden worktable and a pantry. I bought a small fridge. Adjoining was the "lounge," a large room furnished with a dining table and four wooden chairs, and an 'easy' chair and sofa that resembled old fashioned American lawn furniture, with wooden frames and webbing across the seat and back. Tan cotton cushions made them marginally more comfortable. One bedroom had twin beds, the other a single, all three topped by mattresses stuffed with sisal that rustled as I turned over. I soon bought a better mattress for my own bed. Off the hallway to the bedrooms was a bathroom with its own water heater and a big, deep tub.

Floors throughout were brownish red tile that had to be kept mopped and waxed. Every footprint and bit of grit showed. The windows opened outward rather than upward, the opening covered with a grid of metal bars to keep out thieves. My flat's walls were cinderblock, painted gray inside and pale yellow outside.

I spent the first few nights with another teacher until I could buy furnishings. Puri's, the Indian merchant, or *duka*, in Machakos could make or find just about anything, from liquor to clothing. I bought curtains and lengths of spring coiling with a hook screwed into each end. A Puri employee came to measure my windows and hang curtains, and soon I had privacy.

I bought a saucepan, a skillet, some utensils, stainless steel cutlery, and a set of dishes and glassware, and arranged to have milk and *The East African Standard* delivered every morning. The milk was unhomogenized, and cream rose quickly to the top. I soon learned to scoop it off into a bowl; otherwise it plugged the bottle opening as it cooled.

If I wanted to order anything from Puri's, I put a note in an empty milk bottle, and my order was delivered back at lunchtime. Once a month I got a detailed bill, which I paid by a check in the milk bottle. The system worked wonderfully.

I liked sewing, and the college had sewing machines for the domestic science classes, so I made several dresses. Otherwise, I could have had a local seamstress make them. I could even have bought sandals cut from old automobile inner tubes and stitched up on an ancient Singer as I watched.

We were far enough away from city lights that everything was velvety black at night, and the sky was full of constellations I wasn't familiar with, like the Southern Cross. I'd lie in my bed with the curtains open, looking out, and listening to a tapping sound that I was sure was rain, but for the first months it was always a dry, rasping wind.

A servant came with the house, a man named Kiilu. He showed me his letter of reference, folded until it was falling apart. Kiilu had worked for a military man and did excellent ironing, putting creases in everything, but I had little to iron. I agreed to hire him for a while, but ours was not a good relationship. I wasn't used to having somebody in my house all the time, and he drove me almost crazy. He spoke only Kikamba, not Swahili, so we couldn't communicate well enough for me to explain what I wanted done. After a few weeks I managed to get an interpreter and arranged for Kiilu to come only on Fridays to clean, not cook. I felt sorry for him, as jobs were scarce, but I didn't want to go on with an arrangement that was unsatisfactory for both of us.

The other teachers thought I was crazy to want to prepare my own food. I felt strange being waited on, and I wanted privacy.

Kiilu pulled the mosquito net free from the bed each morning, twisting it up into a huge knot that hung from a hook in the ceiling. At night I'd undo the knot and tuck the net edges under the mattress. When I began having him only for cleaning, I merely slid out of a free spot of the net, smoothed the bed and tucked the open net edge back under the mattress. It worked just as well, and it was a lot quicker to get into bed at night.

I also had a half-time gardener, Muyia, referred to as a shamba boy, although he was married and a father. Muyia hoed my small triangle of dirt, swept up fallen leaves, cut the grass, and attached a hose to my kitchen faucet to water the pitiful little garden. After Kiilu left, Muyia began mopping all the floors without being asked. Perhaps, I thought, he would like to be promoted.

But first, I shared another house servant, John, who was more trouble than Kiilu, but in a far different way.

Chapter 6: Getting Out and Entertaining

Toward the end of my second week at Machakos, Cecily Neville came by and asked how I was getting on.

"Fine," I answered. "Except for the strange work schedule, Africa is better than I was expecting."

"Oh, *this* isn't Africa! Come up in the hills with us this afternoon if you'd like to see what our students come from."

We followed the tarmac beyond town as far as it went, then turned onto a dirt road that rapidly became two rocky tracks up a red hillside. Leaving the car at a coffee tree nursery, we began to climb. I hadn't noticed the altitude until my breath began to come in gasps. We stopped to rest.

"How would you like to climb this hill with a baby and a week's groceries on your back?" Miss Neville asked, and almost as if she'd conjured up the image, an African woman came trudging up the hill, a load of bananas and firewood balanced on her shoulder blades. It was kept in place by a leather strap that dug into her forehead, fitting into a ridge cut by past loads. She wore a gaudy length of cotton, wrapped around just above her breasts, and another cloth held a baby to her back beside the load. The baby lay still although flies crawled about its eyes, nose and mouth. The woman trod stolidly, her hands busily weaving a sisal basket as she walked. As she passed us, she smiled and said, "Jambo, memsahibs."

Miss Anderson and Miss Neville greeted her, but I was too horrified to speak. "How can she live like that?" I asked when she had gone past.

"What else can she do?" Miss Neville asked quietly.

"That's what we're up against," Miss Anderson said. "That woman is probably not more than twenty-five, yet she looks fifty. We must save the next generation from that, and make them women who think and take part in their country. Whenever you feel we're not doing anything important in Africa, remember this."

We walked on, past African huts made of sticks plastered with mud. A few had tin roofs, but most were thatched, and all lacked doors and windows. Naked children played in the dust and men lolled in the shade of banana or coffee trees, ignoring the women who dug in the arid dirt with pangas, their all-purpose long knives.

"Why are they digging?" I asked. "Nothing will grow now."

"They believe the rain will come soon," Miss Neville said. "And they're planting the seed maize to keep from eating it. They're starving, you know."

The next day I went to the local hospital for a check-up, a work requirement in Kenya. I sat uneasily among the African patients on wooden benches on the veranda. Children played silently or whimpered fitfully, the mothers ignoring them. There was no liveliness, none of the energy I'd seen in Mohan's niece and nephew, and no mothers watched proudly to see what their offspring were learning. Don't the mothers *care* that their children have open sores and swollen abdomens? I wondered, and felt angry at them for their neglect and seeming lack of interest.

After my check-up, the doctor took me around the hospital, which he said was very modern. We walked past lying listlessly on cots, patients so thin their bones all showed. The odor of sickness and disinfectant made me want to run. How could he talk so proudly of the hospital?

I became almost a fanatic about health, taking my malaria pills, boiling water and milk, spraying everywhere, scrubbing vegetables and washing them in potassium permanganate as we'd been told to do. I couldn't take a chance of getting sick and going to that hospital.

Teaching practice began. Our students had to go out to local schools to observe, and we had to accompany them. Since I didn't have a car, the principal assigned me to a school two miles away.

I put off going out to my school, Mumbuni, as long as I could, dreading the unfamiliar, feeling a slight shrinking at the thought of being the only European in a whole school of Africans. Finally I made myself pack a lunch and a thermos of coffee and trudge the two miles to Mumbuni.

My spirits lifted during the walk. The beauty of Kenya is irresistible: flat-topped thorn trees, rounded red-clay hills terraced and planted with banana and coffee trees, African huts nestling against the hillsides, majestic rows of purplish jacaranda trees that strewed the ground beneath them with a colored carpet of flowers, and the incomparable Kenya sky.

I passed African children playing naked in front of their huts, children who saw me as something strange: a European who walked as they did instead of driving a car. They looked up from their play and regarded me solemnly, distrustfully, for a moment, then grinned and said, "Jambo," or sometimes "Hello" or even "Goodbye." They had heard a bit of English spoken and knew these were friendly words. I answered "Hello," and as long as I was in sight they kept waving and repeating "Hello."

The school itself reassured me too. Although Kenya was suffering from drought, the headmaster still made an attempt at growing things on the school grounds: flaming red poinsettias, white spider lilies and gently drooping pepper trees. The students tended the plants as part of their agriculture curriculum, digging in the dust with pangas.

The buildings were of homemade brown bricks, the floors cement. The children crowded together on wooden benches and shared the meager supplies, but everything was scrupulously clean, and there was an earnestness about everyone, from headmaster down to the smallest child.

The school, operated by the Africa Inland Mission, taught grades four through seven. In grades one through four the pupils were taught in their tribal language, but studied Swahili and English. Intermediate and secondary schools were taught only in English.

As I waited for the principal, I looked around at his office. It held a table, a chair, and a bookcase. On the table stood what must have been the oldest typewriter in Africa, with a ribbon worn through in places.

He came in, an African over six feet tall, but so thin he couldn't have weighed more than 150 pounds. His coat and trousers hung from him, his white shirt was frayed from countless washings, and he wore no socks. His mildewed shoes were too large, and I knew without seeing the bottoms that they had holes. Yet he was trying to dress as he thought a headmaster should dress, with dignity.

He greeted me with a big smile and outstretched hand, eager to cooperate with me or anyone else who could help Africans get an education. After showing me around the school he left me at the room where Grace, one of my students, was giving a lesson. He was not only the principal but taught 29 class periods per week—8 more than I did. It was humbling.

Grace Teaching at a Primary School in Machakos

The students in Grace's class, already crowded three to a bench, crowded closer so I could sit down. Some of them were children no longer, but bearded young men, still trying to learn. Whenever their parents could raise enough shillings for the school fees, boys and girls attended school. If times were hard and money scarce, they might stay home and work in the shamba or tend the herds.

That day was a turning point for me. I felt ashamed of myself and my country for demanding luxury and comfort in everything. The headmaster and pupils were struggling against weather, poverty and disease, making the best of the situation. The overloaded woman weaving a basket, the mothers at the clinic, the doctor, and our students were also doing that, with a patience so immense that to Americans it seemed not patience but resignation.

The girls walked with me back to the college after they finished teaching for the day, and on the way discussed their teaching problems. "Miss, what can we do about the students who are sick?" one asked. "Or too hungry to pay attention?"

What could I say? I'd seen it too: the thin bodies, sores, weak eyes and bad teeth. "I don't know," I admitted. "You can ask the doctor to come for a clinic. The real solution is teaching them to grow better crops and perhaps eating some of their cattle instead of saving it for bride price."

They giggled at that, knowing the importance of those cattle. As educated young women with jobs, their bride price would soar. They would command many cattle.

"It takes time," I went on. "You can't do everything at once."

"No, but we must try, Miss," Grace answered quietly.

Over the next weeks I walked to three different schools to observe and grade my students. I could follow the lesson easily for the students who taught in English, and I thought they were doing a super job. One student, Phyllis, taught a history lesson, drew a map on the board, summarized, and had the students copy notes. I gave her an A. Another showed her pupils how to make jump ropes from sisal and used them in a P.E. lesson. Such lessons were easy to grade.

One student taught primary children in Kikamba, and even though I couldn't understand a word she said, I could see that the children were learning. She drew quite recognizable figures on the board, representing a cow (*nzau*), a hut (*nyumba*), and several rabbits (*mwaazimu*), and wrote their Kikamba names underneath, pronouncing them as she went. The children watched eagerly, raised their hands to answer, and chanted alphabet sounds and words along with her. Then she made simple sentences using each new word. I gave her an A too.

At the end of the teaching practice, examiners came out from Nairobi to observe all students who received A, and all who were in danger of failing. Phyllis they concluded taught stereotyped lessons. I had overgraded her, but she passed easily with a B and was pleased.

In between teaching and observing, I got acquainted with the Machakos area. The town was ringed by the Muwa Hills, brown and sere in the drought, but beautiful when I saw the sun come up quickly at seven, silhouetting them stark and black against an orange sky.

Between the college and town was a small stone church, where four Protestant denominations alternated Sundays holding services. A much bigger Catholic church in Machakos itself, rather than having a service only once a month, had frequent Masses conducted by two priests.

To the northeast was the market, where I walked one day with Kiilu, to his disgust. I wanted to see where he went when he shopped for vegetables, why it took him half a day to make the trip, and if I were paying the right price for what he bought. We reached the market in fifteen minutes. All around us, under a makeshift sunshade, Africans had spread their wares on burlap or on the bare, dusty earth: pineapples, scrawny tomatoes, baskets, trays, wooden carvings, live chickens trussed with string, eggs, and heaps of potatoes, onions and carrots. As I approached, they beseeched, "Memsahib! Memsahib!" I had given Kiilu five shillings. I indicated that I wanted carrots and potatoes, and let him bargain. I didn't want to try bargaining until my Swahili was better. Kiilu bought the vegetables at a good price and I let him keep the remainder of the money.

Machakos even had industry: the coffee factory, and Kenya Orchards. The coffee berries weren't roasted at Machakos, only gathered, sorted, dried and bagged. Kenya Orchards, though, made jam on the premises. Tins passed down a long conveyor belt, great vats steamed fragrantly, and at the back of the main building lay a huge heap of pineapple peel rotting sweetly in the sunshine.

In the town proper, a series of brown brick buildings housed the law courts, the District Commissioner's Office, the post office, a police post, a branch of Barclay's Bank and even a little movie theater that alternated Asian and European—mostly American—movies. Puri's stood among a cluster of flimsy, temporary-looking shops. From this hub overloaded buses lumbered out in various directions, trailing blue diesel smoke. On the outskirts were the Italian Garage, for car repairs, and the hospital, for people repairs. Machakos had about all I needed to function, except a social life.

Surgit wrote regularly, but he was in Kampala, four hundred miles away. In late September, Mohan called. Surgit had warned me that Mohan was a playboy, but when he invited me to go to Nyeri, I accepted. Nyeri was in Kikuyu country, near Mt. Kenya, the snow-capped mountain on the Equator. We came back by Thika, where Jomo Kenyatta made a victory parade that the *Standard* estimated attracted a crowd of 150,000. Perhaps 500 were Asians and a dozen had pale faces like mine. All the others were triumphant Kikuyu. Kenyatta's truck and the others in the parade, decorated in tree branches and banners in the Uhuru colors of red, green and white, passed swiftly through town. I snapped a quick photo of the Kenyan hero waving to the crowd.

Kenyatta arrives at Thika

Surgit wrote that he was coming to Nairobi for the Royal Show, an agricultural fair. The day his letter arrived, however, the office clerk brought a note saying Surgit had called, and couldn't come to Kenya for the weekend after all. I was disappointed, as I was looking forward to seeing him again. I'd made chocolate cupcakes to serve, and in my disappointment, I ate half a dozen of them.

Another teacher also invited me to the Royal Show, but I couldn't go anyway. I was an "invigilator," which meant an exam observer or monitor, on Royal Show day.

A few days later Mrs. Bubole took me to the sports club and introduced me, and I was offered immediate membership. The Machakos Sports Club, for Europeans only, had tennis courts, golf, archery, a squash court, a tiny library, a dance floor, a well-stocked bar and a slot machine that paid a lot of the club's expenses. The club was housed in a low white-painted wooden building facing the golf course and pasture that led to MTC.

A sign in the club said, "Coat and tie required after five." No mention was made about long pants or socks. I saw men come in from sports in shorts and tennis shoes, go into the locker room and come out wearing a tweed jacket over their sports togs, pulling a crumpled tie from the pocket.

I've never been interested in sports or much good at them, but I joined the club. It was the place to go in Machakos, and I wanted to fit in.

There was also allegedly an Asian club, but I never saw it. The African club I could hear, and the music that poured forth at night sounded livelier than the European club's.

I needed a car, so when a faculty member leaving the country wanted to sell her VW, I decided to take a look at it. Kenya's civil service would lend me the money for the car if it passed inspection, or "vetting." Miss Anderson drove me and the car into Nairobi and we shopped while it was being vetted. It didn't pass, so I didn't buy it. I wondered later how different my life would have been if I'd bought it anyway without a loan. I had enough money in the bank at home from the sale of my car there.

One day in early October a woman and a child knocked on my door, and the woman said, "Hi, I'm Beje Oliver," in what was clearly an American voice, and a Southern one at that. "This is my daughter Kim. We've just moved into the next house." Thus began a friendship that has lasted forty years. Beje and I talked books and had tea, and played tennis equally badly. Kim became my little shadow, chatting with me in a very grown-up fashion.

Beje's husband Chad was an anthropologist from the University of Texas on a project in Kenya, and a published western and science fiction writer. Because of lack of housing in the area, they'd arranged to live in one of the vacant flats on our campus.

Beje had a houseboy named John, who had worked for them when they lived briefly in a house on a sisal plantation. She didn't need or want a full-time servant anymore than I did, so we decided to share John.

The following Wednesday I went with the Olivers into Nairobi, where we discovered The Supermarket, and went wild buying things I hadn't found in Machakos: aluminum foil, Brillo pads, dishwashing liquid, and corn on the cob. The Africans ate the corn almost hard, calling it 'mealies.' I could see why it wasn't popular with Europeans. We had dinner at the Norfolk Hotel, a lovely old place once frequented by Ernest Hemingway and other celebrities.

That Sunday I had invited Mohan to lunch. I heard a car drive up and looked out the window to see Surgit getting out. Surgit! He hadn't said he was coming.

"I decided last night to come," he explained. "I'm sorry I couldn't make it last week, and I really wanted to see you. I drove all night and slept a few hours with friends in Nairobi. Let's go somewhere for lunch."

"Why didn't you call?" I asked.

"I couldn't call the college so late, and I wanted to surprise you. Aren't you glad to see me?"

I tried to be. I smiled and hugged him before I told him Mohan was coming for lunch.

He looked stunned.

About that time Mohan drove up and came in laden with gifts: a pork roast, a stack of new magazines and the Sunday paper, a bag of oranges, one of apples, a box of grapes and two boxes of strawberries. I thanked him profusely. He'd undoubtedly recognized Surgit's car, but I told him, "Surgit's here. He came unexpectedly."

Mohan and Surgit gave each other a brief hug and then chatted in Gujerati while I finished up dinner. I have no idea what they said; probably deciding which one should leave first.

Mohan left right after lunch, conceding the field to Surgit, who took a nap while I cleared up.

That evening, as tired as he was, Surgit took me into Nairobi for dinner and a movie. There was no restaurant in Machakos, and he couldn't go to the club with me. We could have stayed at my flat and talked and eaten leftovers for dinner, but we had little to talk about except what fun we'd had together in Kampala.

He took another nap, and left a little after one. When I heard his footsteps fade away on the sidewalk, I was ashamed of myself that I hadn't been gladder to see him.

Life is full of 'ifs.' If he'd come another weekend things might have been different. If I'd been assigned near Kampala, we'd probably have kept on dating. I was the alien there, but Kampala was cosmopolitan and multiracial and we made an attractive, lively couple. Machakos had become my world, and he was the alien, and Kampala was too far away for us to see each other often. It was over.

Mohan Gill at Thika

I knew Mohan only took me out to have a companion for dinners and concerts in Nairobi. Indian women didn't date and Mohan didn't want to go out alone. But Surgit? Why would he drive four hundred miles if he didn't care for me? He never said, and I never asked him. Maybe I didn't want to know.

Chapter 7: Romance

My first date with a European in Kenya lasted the half hour it took him to drive a few miles toward Nairobi, make a racist remark and for me to call him a bigot. He turned back toward Machakos, dropped me off at my flat and never spoke to me again.

Next I met Don at the club with the Olivers, we played tennis, and he seemed amusing. He joked about his car license. In East Africa, the plates began with the letter for the country: U for Uganda, K for Kenya, etc., plus a couple more letters and two or three numbers. His was KAT 99. He said he could never leave work early or sneak off anywhere without someone saying, "I saw you on Tuesday noon." He invited me for drinks and dinner in Nairobi along with two other couples. All went well until we got back to my flat. He came in without being asked, and began pawing me. When I objected, he said, "So you think I'm a dirty old man, don't you?"

"You're not that old," I said, and sent him off. I decided I should concentrate on teaching, not dating.

That vow changed when the faculty were invited to a party at the Machakos Arms, given by the bachelors who lived there. I went with Beje Oliver and Kim, while Chad was out in the field on a research project.

The Machakos Arms was a series of round, mud-brick *bandas* with thatched roofs, set in a cluster of eucalyptus trees around a central lobby and dining room. The courtyard and parking area were dusty red dirt.

That night I met the two men who were to dominate my life for the rest of my time in Kenya.

As we drove up and Beje parked the Land Rover, a tall, elegant blond man walked up and spoke to her. My God, he's handsome, I thought.

"You can put Kim in our banda," he said.

'Our' implied sharing with someone. He's married, I concluded dismally. But it figures. Anybody who looks like that and has such good manners, even showing consideration for a child, is bound to be married. So I merely smiled when Beje said, "Emilee, this is Ray Goodwin."

We went in to join a raucous crowd. Chubby Checker's "Let's Twist Again" was playing. Someone asked me to dance, and as I moved out onto the floor, I saw Beje and Ray watching. Where's his wife? I wondered. Maybe dancing with somebody else. It hadn't taken long to figure out what people meant by a 'Kenya marriage.' Both parties felt free to have affairs. Unlike most societies, Kenya's worked out to the advantage of women, as there was a surplus of men.

The room was full of single men in their late twenties and early thirties who danced. I was definitely going to have a good time.

The evening flew by. There was some kind of round, and Ray was briefly my partner. He towered over me, smiling and serene, and we moved well together.

"Boy, you're tall," I said gracelessly.

"Six five. Everyone asks," he answered in a beautiful English voice.

"Do you have children?" I asked.

He looked puzzled. "Why, no."

Before I could ask anything else, we had to change partners again.

My next partner was also blond, but as different from Ray as could be. He was only a couple of inches taller than I, very muscular and vigorous. He had a head of curly hair, and he laughed a lot. "I'm Enrico," he said, and added an Italian last name I didn't understand and couldn't repeat. "And you must be Miss Hines." He pronounced 'Miss' like "Meese". "I am at the cement plant at Athi River." Then he too was gone.

When we broke for supper, a forestry officer invited me to sit with him. To go with the buffet was a strange drink, shandy, made by mixing beer and lemonade together. It was dreadful.

Suddenly one of the police officers came in and told Beje, "You'd better get out to the banda and rescue your child. *Siafu* are everywhere."

"What are siafu?" I asked the forestry officer, who was pushing back his plate. I imagined an attack of a cult.

"Huge ants," he said, heading for the door.

Soon Beje, Ray, and the others were back.

"Is Kim all right?" I asked.

"Yes. Fortunately Ray had tucked in the mosquito net. It was covered with ants, but she's all right," Beje said. "She slept right through it. Still, I think I'd better take her home."

The next day Beje came over at teatime and suggested we put our food together for supper.

When I agreed, she said, "I've invited Ray too. He seems interested."

"In me? What about his wife?"

"What made you think he was married?"

When I told her, she just laughed. "Not married, never married. A bit shy," she said.

Dinner went well, and afterward Beje put Kim to sleep and we adults played poker until 1 a.m.

Ray, I saw, was no poker player. At least, not that night. He paid little attention to the cards. Every time I looked at him, he was looking at me, and he'd smile. He had perfectly chiseled features, intense blue eyes and an almost innocent manner. I found out later what a life he'd led: evacuated from London to the country as a child during the blitz, then brought back as the worst of the bombing began. He'd won scholarships to a 'good public school,' as the British call their private schools, and to university. He'd gone with the British army to fight in Malaya and then been sent to Kenya to help put down Mau Mau. When that was over, he'd joined the Kenya police. He'd seen violence and atrocities, but had been seemingly untouched by it.

A few days later the Olivers, Ray and I went to Nairobi shopping. I loved Nairobi, despite my first unpleasant encounter.

As we made the turn from Machakos onto the Mombasa-Uganda road we'd sometimes catch a glimpse of Kilimanjaro floating on the horizon off to the south. At Athi River the huge Kenya Meat Commission building stood high on the left, and from there to Nairobi we often saw animals beside the road, especially giraffe. The entrance to the Royal Game Park came next and then the airport. There the roundabouts started, traffic circles planted with brilliant bougainvillea. We'd make our way around to the left and continue into the city on Queen Elizabeth Way.

Soon we were heading down Government Road, lined with jacaranda trees, pausing for people on the white-painted crosswalks called 'zebras,' and finally turning into Delamere Avenue, which fronted the New Stanley Hotel.

The Thorn Tree, the hotel's outdoor cafe, was the meeting place for everyone in East Africa. United Nations troops in khaki uniforms and pale blue berets, on leave from the Congo, would be at one table having a beer or coffee with hot milk; African politicians would be chatting at another; and at others, housewives would be consulting shopping lists over tea. Movie stars and other celebrities made safaris to Kenya and came to The Thorn Tree. One day Beje and I spoke to the actor Edward G. Robinson there having a drink, and another day we spotted William Holden. Announcements requested, "Sir So-and-So, please come to the front desk for a call." It was the crossroads of the world.

Me with Ray Goodwin

That day I only paid attention to Ray. He helped me choose a camera, my first that made slides, and had a light meter, interchangeable lens, and all the other gimmicks.

The following Friday Ray took me to the New Stanley for their fantastic buffet lunch. His friend Mike joined us, and I enjoyed their good humor and the place itself. Coping with the array of silverware kept me busy. I knew to start at the outside and work inwards. The two pieces laid crosswise above my plate were for dessert, I discovered. The fish knife was something new, broader than the dinner knife but pointed at the tip to separate out bones. I even managed to eat with my fork in my left hand as they did, without spilling anything.

After lunch we shopped the Municipal Market, and I came away loaded down with fragrant fruits and an armful of flowers.

One evening soon after, we went to The Pagoda for Chinese food. Nairobi had almost anything I could want.

On the Olivers' ninth wedding anniversary, the four of us went to the Equator Club in Nairobi to celebrate.

Beje and Chad Oliver

The Equator Club was famous, and exotic. Papyrus reeds covered the ceiling, and framed Kenya scenes alternated on the walls with African masks and Masai shields: huge cowhide ovals painted in ochre, black and white. The booths were covered in animal skins and the bar in python skin. The top-notch African band wore zebra printed shirts and played the latest dance tunes.

The feature that night was Joe Bundy, billed as the Jamaican Louis Armstrong. He sang Satchmo's songs, and we clapped along with "When the Saints Go Marching In."

The floor show was fun, but the attraction that night for me was dancing with Ray. He was tall, but he was a strong, graceful leader who could guide me through intricate steps. And I'm not known as a follower.

Ray had driven his car, and on the way back he passed the keys to Chad, who promptly ground the gears when he shifted. Ray winced. He was proud of his DKW with the delicate manual transmission, but after he explained again to Chad how to shift, we settled into the backseat and he slid his arm around me.

I knew he was going to kiss me, and I wanted him to. He was a world-class kisser. We exchanged desultory conversation with the Olivers, who pretended to look straight ahead, but mainly we focused on each other. The forty miles to Machakos passed quickly.

The next day at teatime Ray arrived with bad news. He'd been posted to Lokitaung, seven hundred miles away on the Ethiopian border, as far from Machakos as he could get and still be in Kenya.

"Once I'd have welcomed a chance to get up there, but that was before I met you," he said. "Now I don't want to leave Machakos."

"What will you do there?" I asked.

"Try to keep the tribes from killing each other. Disarm them if we can. Actually, their weapons are probably more dangerous to the man holding it than to anybody in front of the barrel. Some of them go back to the first World War."

"I wish you weren't going."

"I'll miss you," he said.

"When do you leave?"

"Day after tomorrow, early. Will you write to me? Mail only goes out from there once a week, but I'll have a letter for you on every lorry that leaves."

I promised. We spent the next day together, photographing scenes around Machakos while I learned to use my new camera. He brought along a tape recorder and had me sing some calypso songs and pop tunes, and then we recorded some conversation.

"I'm going to play this when I'm off the Frontier and imagine I'm with you and you're singing for me and talking with me," he said.

Finally he said goodbye just before dawn, and went to the Machakos Arms to pack. I drank two cups of strong coffee and taught my classes all day without remembering a word I said.

Chapter 8: The Floods

With Ray gone, I focused on the college, which took a lot of my time. One faculty meeting went on from 4:30 to 6:30, and another the next day was almost as long. I earned an extra $20 grading papers for a national exam, and got my own mid-term exams graded and recorded.

And still I heard the dry, rattling wind and saw more bleached bones in pastures on the way to Nairobi.

Finally the rain came, faint and tentative at first, so that even old-timers hardly trusted that it was real and not another trick of nature that had fooled them for three years.

But this rain was real. It rained at least once every day, for an hour or more. The air no longer dried my skin, and the cracked pasture between the college and the club began to heal, sprouting a new cover of green grass. After the rain stopped each day, a glorious rainbow appeared, arching completely across the sky. When I was a child, my mother used to say that there was a pot of gold at the end of the rainbow, but we could never see the end, only a curved center. In Kenya, the rainbow ended between the college and the club.

Letters from home described an early November snow in the mountains, and the last sales of the tobacco crop. I missed my family, and I could envision autumn on the farm with an almost painful homesickness, but I was busy and involved in Kenya.

I planted watermelon, green bean and flower seeds I'd smuggled from the States. Everything came up quickly, but locals predicted the watermelons wouldn't ripen because of the altitude.

During the second week of rain we had Parents' Day, attended by whole families. The Domestic Science classes made sandwiches, cakes and tea, and the physical education classes practiced Scottish dances to perform for the visitors. Girls paraded in dresses they'd made in sewing classes and Jerseys (sweaters) they'd knitted.

Visitors sloshed from building to building in the mud. In the afternoon we had assembly in three languages. Miss Shrubsole spoke in English, followed by murmurs and appreciative laughter. Then a Wakamba student would translate into Kikamba and another set of parents would murmur and laugh. Finally, a Swahili-speaker from one of the coastal tribes translated into her language.

We lecturers had Open House in our flats afterward. Several students brought guests to meet me. If I knew for sure they were Wakamba, I'd greet them "Nuvoo." If I wasn't sure, I'd say "Jambo," the Swahili greeting. No bent-over women such as I'd seen in the hills came to the gathering. Our students were the privileged ones, whose parents could afford school fees and bus fare to Machakos.

More rain came, more in three weeks than Kenya had seen in the past two years. My shoes stayed wet and laundry took days to dry. Low places on campus became broad shimmering pools. The paved road to Nairobi was passable, but the murram roads became bogs, including the main road to the coast. Isolated groups of Africans who a month earlier had been given food because of drought were now lining up for drops of maize because floods kept supply lorries from coming through.

One day the District Commissioner's helicopter landed on the pasture between us and the club. Within seconds of arrival, it was mobbed by people who thought it brought free food. Instead, the DC was only investigating flood damage. Gradually the crowd dispersed, running as the sweep of helicopter rotors swirled loose debris.

Washed out bridge at Athi River

A pleasant interlude during the floods was dinner for the Hindi New Year's Day with Zaida Deen, a part-time faculty member, and her husband, Jan Mohammed Deen Puri. His father owned Puri's and subsidized the cinema in Machakos.

Mrs. Deen, exotic and lovely in a red sari and gold sandals, played a stringed instrument like a harp, her fingers long and graceful, and sang Indian songs. The evening passed quickly and I ate too many fattening Indian desserts.

One morning when the milk and newspaper were delivered, I read that two trains had plunged into swollen streams between us and Mombasa, ripping up the rails as they fell and cutting off transport with the coast. In the other direction, two bridges on the main roads over the Athi River had washed out, torn from the cement moorings at both ends. A road from Nairobi northward had crumbled, causing an avalanche of earth that destroyed an African home and killed five people.

We still had rail connections to Nairobi, but for how long? Mail, newspapers and food were brought by train across Athi River, then loaded onto waiting lorries on our side for distribution. Because so much food was grown in our district, Ukambani, we in Machakos were not in danger of starvation, but by mid-November, Mombasa had been without meat and fresh milk for two weeks. As the floods continued, Kenya ceased to be a unified country and became instead a series of isolated settlements.

The American Consulate sent telegrams saying that in case of emergency, we would be evacuated, but we Americans just laughed. Unless they came on helicopters, there was no way to rescue us, and the helicopters all seemed to be bringing in government observers. When a second one landed on the pasture carrying only people and no food supplies, angry Africans attacked it and practically tore it apart before the police used tear gas to disperse the mob and the helicopter could take off. The British and American air forces organized food drops.

Downstream from Athi River village, a causeway could be crossed briefly each day when the water receded. One Wednesday, the Olivers and I waited in line for over an hour along with a bus, several lorries, and half a dozen other cars.

A group of Masai warriors, majestic in dark red cloaks and great beaded earrings, stood leaning one-legged on their spears watching us, probably speculating on what the *Mzungi* (Europeans) needed so badly in Nairobi that they could not wait until the floods were over. The patient Masai were used to waiting for months for the few items they needed from civilization. Mostly they lived by drinking milk mixed with cow's blood, and their homes were rude *kraals* made with sticks and brush held together by a mixture of mud and dung. Floods scarcely disrupted their lives and were even a blessing, making more grass grow for their cattle.

In one of the infrequent mail deliveries, I had a note from our program coordinator from Columbia, saying he was coming to observe my teaching. As the day approached, I didn't think I'd be observed, since rain continued to fall and roads remained impassable.

I was relieved that he hadn't shown up for one of my domestic science disasters. Two such incidents stick in my mind. On breadmaking day, two girls claimed the same baked loaf. "I put my mark there!" one claimed, pointing to an indentation in the bread. "I put *my* mark just there!" the other argued, pointing to another indentation. I settled it by cutting the loaf in half. When all the loaves were claimed but one, I sliced it in half also, and the two claimants shared it. I never knew which girl was wrong, but they both received the same grade, and they each had two half-loaves of homemade bread to eat.

Making scrambled eggs was my mistake. The electric stove took ages to heat, and wasn't hot enough to make the eggs fluffy when we added them to the skillet. As the student stirred, the eggs thickened and turned gluey. "Do Europeans like scrambled eggs?" they asked doubtfully, observing the yellow mess. If that had been my introduction to them, I wouldn't have.

On the appointed day for the coordinator's visit, I was conducting a tutorial—a small group discussion—with my domestic science class when the office clerk knocked on my door to say a visitor was on his way.

I alerted the girls to participate and ask questions. This man was grading my teaching as I had been grading theirs. They understood. The examiner. They wanted me to get a good mark. The lesson went smoothly, with lots of questions. Afterward, over tea, I admitted that I hadn't really expected him.

He said he'd driven from Nairobi to Athi River with his wife and another couple, walked the rail line, and hired a driver on our side to bring them to Machakos. He planned to spend the night at the boys' school next door and head back to Nairobi the same way the next day. What dedication!

Sufurias set outside the dining hall to catch water after our water system washed away, 1961

The rains continued, and the pipes bringing water to the college washed away. Nothing came when we turned on the faucets, but lots of water was coming from the sky. The students put out vessels to catch water, and our house servants dipped water from the cement storm drains that criss-crossed the campus to fill our bathtubs for flushing toilets. For water to drink and use in cooking, we set our pots and pans along the sidewalks beside our houses, where the rain came off the roof. Unnecessary bathing was postponed.

Pots and pans began to disappear, and one night a pair of gumboots was taken from a teacher's car. We had a thief in our midst. Strangely, nothing of mine or Beje's was taken.

We all wanted the rain to stop, but when it did, there would be a time before the water system was back in operation. Then the servants would have to bring water from the lake between us and the club—water polluted with sewage and cow dung that would have to be boiled and filtered.

The British army came to our rescue, bringing barrels of water to the campus and helping to distribute it fairly.

In the midst of this, I continued teaching and taking my turn at evening and Sunday afternoon duty.

One evening a student roused me to say that another was 'velly, velly sick,' shaking and cold. I pulled on my raincoat and boots and went over to the dormitory. I could tell that the student was indeed very sick, and sent for the van driver to take her to the local hospital. She was admitted, and I got home about midnight. It was malaria, the fourth case of the term, but the first on my watch. We also had three cases of mumps, but none when I was on duty. I never had mumps as a child, and I thought how ironical it would be if instead of some dread tropical disease I got mumps in Africa.

I went two weeks without mail from the States, and three weeks without hearing from Ray, but I knew floods had reached desert Lokitaung as well as Machakos. In one of his letters that finally arrived, he said the mail lorry had overturned in the mud. Ray wouldn't have gotten my letters, and might be feeling as forlorn as I was.

Several things happened then, all related. The rain let up, and the students' dance was scheduled. Since I had to be a chaperone, I decided to invite a partner and dance. I'd seen Enrico at the club since meeting him at the Machakos Arms party six weeks before, so I invited him.

The students were thrilled to see a faculty member dressed up and dancing with a man, and they smiled and giggled at us.

Rico invited me to go with him and two Italian families waterskiing the next day at a lake—which people referred to as a 'dam'—near Nairobi, where he had a boat. I'd only water-skied twice before, so when I succeeded in making it around the lake without falling, I stopped while I was ahead, feeling pretty proud of myself.

Rico entered a water-skiing competition that afternoon, going up a ramp and dropping about five feet to the water. He'd never gone off a ramp before, but decided he might as well try it for a competition. Up the ramp he went and dropped to the water below with a smack that threw him off the skis. He wasn't the only daredevil. One skier who went off the ramp successfully had only one leg!

Enrica, one of the Italian women, laughed and said Rico was crazy. "Once he jumped out of a plane into this lake on a bet," she said. "He won the case of beer, but he was in hospital two weeks. Another time he walked around the top of a big factory chimney." That should have warned me about Rico's wildness, but was just someone to pass time with until Ray came back.

I spent a good part of the day with Enrica, her husband Mario and their two children. When Rico wasn't skiing, he was driving the boat to pull other skiers. One of them was Marian, a sleek, tanned blonde in a white swimsuit.

When prizes were awarded, she grabbed her cup and ran to hug and kiss Rico. When she left, he said, "You mustn't be jealous of her. She is someone I used to date."

I wasn't jealous where he was concerned. Of her skiing ability, her bronze tan and great body? Yes, a bit.

Afterward, we went to a soccer match, and then for curry supper. The Italians spoke English—Enrica's husband Mario had been an Italian prisoner of war in Kenya—but usually chatted in Italian. Because of studying Spanish, I could understand some Italian.

Rico asked me out for the following Wednesday. He was late arriving, and while I waited for him, I worked on lesson plans, and realized I needed to talk to Hazel Bak, another teacher. I went across to her house and knocked on her front door, but got no answer. As I came back around the house, a figure was climbing out of her kitchen window: John, the house servant I had begun sharing with Beje!

I was too startled to be frightened. "John!" I managed to say. "What are you doing in Mrs. Bak's house?"

"I was visiting her houseboy," he said, a totally illogical answer. The houseboy would have opened the door for him, and nobody ever visited or left by a window.

Before I could say anything more, he dropped to the ground and ran.

I went to the Assistant Principal's flat and said, "There's something I have to tell you right now. In the morning I'll probably think I dreamed it."

The AP roused the night watchman, who with his dog went to stand guard. Hazel was spending the night in Nairobi, she said. With the master key she unlocked Hazel's door, and there on the kitchen floor was a big cloth bundle like cartoons showed burglars carrying. Tied inside one of Hazel's new sheets were her camera, silverware and new clothing. The AP relocked the house, and at first light called the police and waited for Hazel.

Stupidly, John came to work that morning, and this time I *was* frightened. I slipped out to tell the AP, and within a few minutes the police came and arrested John in my kitchen. As he was led away, his eyes red with rage, he screamed that I was lying.

We now knew why Beje's and my pots and pans were not stolen. John wouldn't have had anything to work with otherwise. And if Rico had been on time for our date, I wouldn't have caught John in the act.

I had to testify against John in court. He was found guilty and sentenced to two years' on the road work detail. He would still be in prison when I left Kenya at the end of my contract, and I saw him occasionally on the way from the college into Machakos.

John told the labor officer that I hadn't paid him his wages, and that I was angry because he'd broken a dish. Fortunately, someone had warned me when I first arrived to keep a notebook of wages paid, write down the date and amount and have the servant sign it. I showed the labor officer my notebook with John's signatures, and that was that.

Rain brought plagues, and I could relate to Moses. Locusts hatched, and for a week hopped everywhere. They were crushed in doors, flattened in books, stepped on wherever people walked. Then there were frogs, about an inch across and almost translucent. Instead of the crunch of locusts, we felt the squish of squashed frogs underfoot.

Then Beje discovered another East African pest. Her big toe swelled so painfully she could just hobble around. "It's a jigger. Have your houseboy pick it out with a knife," old hands advised. Instead, she went into Nairobi to a doctor, who took a knife and picked out three jiggers and three egg sacs. Jiggers live in dirt, get under people's fingernails and toenails and lay eggs. The hatchlings eat away the flesh around them.

The rains finally ended, along with the college term. Again the British army came to the rescue, taking the students home in army lorries, this time because of a transport strike.

The frangipani beside my back door blossomed with fragrant white blooms. Mail arrived, bringing three letters from Ray. Ever since he'd left for the frontier, we'd counted on his being back in Machakos for Christmas, but it was not to be. Again circumstances were playing havoc with our relationship. He'd still be in the NFD at Christmas, he wrote, but in January we could go to the coast for a week and get to know each other better. It sounded great to me.

Me and Rico on his boat at Nairobi Dam

Chapter 9: Christmas in Kenya

With the college closed until late January, I could get ready for Christmas. I'd invited Joan and Gene, TEA friends, to spend Christmas at Machakos with me.

The Sunday before Christmas, I went with the Olivers to the Protestant church in Machakos for a community carol singing and afterward to the club for a buffet supper. On December 18 we went into Nairobi, and decided ahead of time to stay overnight at the New Stanley. Mohan had invited us all to dinner, and getting back to Machakos late might be a problem if it rained again.

Soon after we arrived at Mohan's, he had a phone call and came back into the lounge to announce, "My father has just arrived from Mombasa. I must go to the airport to collect him. The houseboy will fix whatever you want to drink, and I'll return soon." He seemed a bit uneasy.

The houseboy fed Kim and Mohan's niece and nephew, and their mother ate with them and put them all to bed while we snacked on cashews and spicy Indian treats.

We speculated about what the father would be like. I'd heard so much about the patriarch that I was in awe of him. He was one of the richest men in East Africa, and had a large office building and a street in Nairobi named for him.

We heard the door open and then Mohan came in and said, "Father, I'd like you to meet my American friends."

Mr. Gill was charming. He bowed and smiled when he was introduced to each of us, and chatted all evening in perfect, British-accented English about world events and the future of East Africa. He had a long white beard and wore a turban and a loose white cotton suit rather like pajamas.

Mr. Gill was a vegetarian, and while we had chicken curry, he ate only vegetables and rice. We all finished the meal with fruit and *rosgullas*, small balls of milk curd deep-fried and floating in a sugar syrup.

At the New Stanley the next morning I had breakfast in bed, though it wasn't nearly as glamorous as it's depicted in the movies. The breakfast—papaya, thick undercooked bacon, a fried egg, and baked beans—was cold by the time it got to my room, and the toast in Kenya always arrived cold, standing in little drying racks. Accompanying it was a tiny bowl of butter balls lying on crushed ice, difficult enough to spread on hot toast and impossible on cold toast.

Chad tried to forego the morning tea altogether and instead go to the dining room for hot coffee, but signs on the door in Swahili and English—"Hapana Chai, No Tea"—did no good. The tea tray always arrived.

We did Christmas shopping. Beje and I each ordered a turkey at six shillings a pound, then about 90 cents. The fifteen-pound turkey thus cost almost as much as my rent for a month. We found cans of cranberry sauce and cornmeal for cornbread stuffing. Then, wandering down a side street, I saw an amazing sign in the window of a tiny Indian grocer: "Picans (American nuts)." I bought two pounds at over a dollar a pound, and rushed to find Beje to show my purchase. She went back to buy two pounds as well, and we laughed at the sign and helped the grocer correct the spelling. After we left, though, he didn't need the sign nearly as much. We'd bought nearly half his stock.

I spent the next few days cooking, and then Christmas began. Joan and Gene arrived on his motorcycle on Thursday.

**Gene Ashby on his motorcycle
(photo by Sharon Hartmann)**

"When are we going to meet this Ray you've been writing about?" Gene asked.

"You won't. His leave has been postponed."

"What a bummer," he said, and I agreed.

On Friday night I'd invited the Italian group to dinner, as Rico had taken me to their house several times. All nine came, counting Rico, who arrived late. The three of us made twelve. I'd rented a punchbowl and glasses from Puri's. I had a punchbowl of chilled burgundy to start, but the Italians arrived with three bottles of wine—chianti, rosatello and champagne.

Dinner was going quietly, a bit strained, until Rico arrived with a bottle of wine and a package of prosciutto. "I came straight here from work," he announced. "Madonna, have I worked today!" The tempo of the party picked up.

Afterward we went to Mario and Enrica's for coffee and brandy. I felt as if I'd been adopted by a family, and Rico was the liveliest member. He laughed and joked, played records, and danced with all the women and girls.

The next morning Gene asked, "Where did you find this Latin lover?"

"I met him at a party, the same night I met Ray."

"You'd better watch out. This guy's used to taking what he wants, and I think he wants you."

We were just getting up on Christmas Eve morning when another TEA teacher arrived. I cooked breakfast and made coffee for everybody, and as we were finishing breakfast Rufus Sanders, a TEA teacher assigned to the boys' school, walked across the pasture to visit, and two other TEA teachers on their way from Makerere to Mombasa stopped in for food and a rest stop.

Chad came over to say Beje's turkey smelled strange. "Would you come and sniff it? I don't think there's any question it's spoiled, but she wants another opinion."

"Sure," I said.

As we went across to their flat, he glanced back at the conglomerate in my lounge and muttered, "I'm sure glad I'm not young anymore."

The minute I stepped into the Olivers' flat, I agreed with Chad. The turkey was spoiled. As it cooked, it filled the flat with a bad odor. What if mine were also spoiled? It was waiting in another teacher's fridge. My fridge was too small, and she was going to be away for several weeks.

"If my turkey is okay, come over and have Christmas dinner with us," I said. "If it's spoiled, we'll open a couple of cans of corned beef or send to Puri's for curry."

After supper we piled into the Olivers' Land Rover, picked up the Machakos Italians, and drove around town Christmas caroling. The Italians sang several songs, then we Americans did, and finally we settled on "Adeste Fideles," which we all knew in Latin. Afterward, we went to the club, and Bill Jones tactfully said he'd go back to the college with the Olivers and have a chat with Chad and an early bedtime. As a black American, he couldn't go to the European club.

At midnight Joan, Gene, the Italians and I went to Mass at the Catholic church. We were a dozen Europeans kneeling with three hundred Africans, for a service in Latin and Kikamba, but however strange it seemed, it was Christmas Eve halfway around the world. I had to remind myself that Christ was born in a place such as Machakos, a place of warm starry nights and dusty roads, not in snowy North America.

From church we went to Mario and Enrica's house for coffee and *galani*, strips of sweet dough crisp fried and sprinkled with sugar. We finally got back to my flat at five a.m. I slid the turkey into the oven and fell into bed.

I awakened hours later to see Rico sitting on the edge of my bed, holding a cup of coffee. "Buon natale, Emilee," he said.

"What?"

"Buon natale. That means Merry Christmas, or actually, good Christmas."

"When did you get here?" I asked fuzzily, reaching for the coffee.

"I slept on your sofa."

I downed the coffee, sent him out and got dressed. I could smell the turkey cooking. It wasn't spoiled, and it smelled wonderful.

Gifts arrived as well as guests. Joan brought me a book, Rico gave me perfume, the Olivers a box of candy and a miniature silver salt & pepper set, and Puri's left a talcum and cologne set when they delivered my Christmas Eve order. My parents' box didn't arrive by Christmas, but a blouse came from my sister, and a box containing waxed paper, plastic wrap, paper towels and aluminum foil from my friend Jo Whitley. About thirty Christmas cards came, and a letter from home. Ray sent a check, part to be given to his cook's wife, who lived near Machakos, and the remainder for me to buy myself a gift. There were no gifts to buy at the Frontier.

I had duty the week after Christmas. During holidays duty included feeding the night watchman's dog, a big bony ridgeback. I had notified Puri's that the dog's bones should be delivered to me for the week, and they were stored in my fridge. The teacher who had duty ahead of me sent over the bag of rice I had to cook for the dog. His name was Bruno, or 'Bluno,' as the Africans pronounced it.

I was awakened in the morning by the night watchman tapping on the door. I dipped half the cooked rice into a *sufuria*, a big metal dish, warmed it briefly over hot water, and set it down for Bruno. He ate it greedily and looked up at me.

"Good dog, Bruno," I said. He stared at me and his tail moved in a tentative wag.

I tried again. "Good Bluno." His tail wagged freely.

"*Mzuri sana*," the night watchman said, grinning so the gaps between his teeth showed. It could mean Bruno was a good dog, Bruno liked the rice, I had picked up quickly on the dog's name, or that things in general were okay.

"Ndio, mzuri," I agreed. He nodded, hitched up the sling that held his bow and arrows, and walked off with Bruno for a snooze, his inner-tube sandals slapping the dusty driveway.

About nine the office clerk came for the keys, and at closing time returned them to me. Mid-morning, I had to check with the office for phone messages or problems that needed attending to.

Just before dark the night watchman and Bruno reported for night duty, and I gave Bruno his bones. At ten I had to make my rounds of the campus with a flashlight. The first few times I did this I knew sheer terror, walking alone on a pitch-black campus, knowing that with my flashlight I was a walking target. But for whom? I soon realized that there were no terrorists out in the pasture, lurking in wait for an unwary teacher.

The guest list shifted. Bill Jones left, and Rich Hawkins arrived, just in time to go to the club for the New Year's Eve costume party. We improvised. Joan wore a muumuu and stuck flowers in her hair, I wore the blue sari Surgit had helped me choose, and Gene just wore a suit. Ron wore sandals and a blanket, carried the bow and arrows I'd purchased for decoration, and went as a night watchman. The magistrate went as Louis XV, complete with plumed hat, lace handkerchief, high-heeled shoes with buckles, and a blue velvet frock coat. The prize went to a farmer dressed as explorer David Livingstone. His family were all his porters, carrying boxes and bales on their heads.

At midnight the settlers lifted their glasses and drank to their last year in Kenya. Many of them planned to sell out and leave when independence came, but nobody knew exactly when that would be. 'Auld Lang Syne' brought a lump to my throat. We were so far from home.

Ron and Gene left, and Joan and I drove into Nairobi to arrange with East African Airways for a 'Flame Lily Holiday' to Rhodesia. Arranging it was almost as time-consuming as getting there. First the airline refused to take a check, so we had to go to the bank and get out 2,990 shillings, about $450, in cash. I drove rapidly to the airline office with the money. Then they said I needed a tax clearance to leave the country, since I'd been earning wages in Kenya and must owe taxes. We called up Inland Revenue and got a waiver, since I had a return ticket and a continuing contract.

Joan at Nairobi Airport

It was almost dark when we landed in Salisbury (now Harare), but we could see enough on the way in from the airport to excite us: skyscrapers, American cars, and roads that had white lines down the center and traffic lights. The shop windows were full of American products. We had little time to enjoy Salisbury, however. Our flight to Kariba left at 5:30 the next morning.

Kariba Dam on the Zambesi River was one of the tallest in the world, and formed what was then the world's largest man-made lake. Our hotel, overlooking the lake, had air-conditioned rooms, the first we'd seen in Africa. We took a boat tour, saw crocodiles, and toured the dam site. The next morning we flew southward the length of the lake to Livingstone. Our plane circled Victoria Falls, dipping the wings so we all had a chance to see and photograph the magnificent falls.

As soon as we checked in at the hotel, Joan and I arranged a van to take us to the falls. We were dropped off beside a huge baobab tree and clambered down a slick wet bank to a spot opposite the falls. The Zambesi spreads out across a wide expanse and pours over the edge into a vast crack in the earth. Mist soaked us right through our raincoats, but we didn't care.

We flew back to Nairobi by way of Ndola in the Congo, a site that had earned its place in history when UN Secretary-General Dag Hammerskold's plane was shot down and he was killed. A storm kept us on the ground over an hour there, so it was after nine when we got back to Nairobi, to that nostalgic sign at the airport showing the distance to the world's major cities. New York was over 7,000 miles away, and home seemed even farther.

I sat in shorts the next day at Machakos reading mail from home that described a snowy Christmas. I still had a week at the coast with Ray to look forward to.

Chapter 10: To the Frontier

Ever since Ray had been sent to the Northern Frontier, I'd counted the days until I could see him again. Twice our plans for a holiday had been thwarted by the Kenya police. They had to consider the safety of the outlying areas, but it seemed unfair that Ray had to be continually kept away.

He wrote that he'd arrive on January 13th, about eight in the evening. He'd spend the night in Machakos, and the next day we'd go to the coast for ten days before my school started again.

About four that afternoon Joan was ironing and I was in the kitchen making a pie from the last of my precious pecans from Christmas.

As soon as I got the pie in the oven, I planned to pick up the clutter around the house and have a bath. Ray was always so immaculate that I wanted everything to be just right when he arrived. I was barefoot, wearing one of my oldest dresses, my hair straggling and limp from the heat.

Suddenly, Ray pulled up outside and came striding toward the kitchen door.

"Hi, you're early," I said inanely.

"We drove straight through from Lokitaung to Nairobi with three drivers and made it in only twenty-three hours," he explained, smiling that smile I remembered so well. "Darling, it's good to see you!"

"I didn't want you to see me this way," I wailed. "I wanted everything to be perfect when you got here."

"You look wonderful to me. I don't mind a bit of flour on your nose. Especially when you're making my favorite pie." He bent to kiss my nose, and pulled me into his arms.

I didn't waste any more time worrying about how I looked. "Bring your things in while I finish this pie. Then have a drink while I get a bath." I poured the filling into the crust, shoved the pie into the oven and cleared the kitchen as quickly as I could, watching through the window as he unloaded his car. He looked as smashing as ever.

I had a record-quick bath, dressed and thrust my feet into sandals, not wanting him to see me barefoot again. My Southern upbringing said barefoot is slovenly.

Ray was talking to Joan, who'd introduced herself and found cashews to go with his drink. She poured a soft drink for herself and one for me, and took hers into the guest room, tactfully leaving us alone.

I set my drink down at the same time Ray set his down, and we met halfway for a welcome-home kiss. I'd forgotten how tall Ray was. He towered over me, the only man in my life who could ever call me a 'sweet little thing' with a straight face. It was wonderful to be with him again.

After a while I said, "Joan's boyfriend was assigned to Mombasa. She wants to ride with us to the coast tomorrow."

He stopped smiling, and I thought for a moment he was angry that I'd invited her to share the car without asking him. Then he said, "We can't go. There's been an armed incursion from Ethiopia and my leave's been canceled. I found out when I got to the Police headquarters in Nairobi. The superintendent tried to get in touch with me at each post, but didn't manage because we didn't stop."

"Not again! They can't do this to you!"

"I'm afraid they can. As long as I'm in the Kenya Police, they control my life. I'm glad I had a chance to get here early. At least I have a few extra hours with you before I have to go back to the NFD."

"It isn't fair. You deserve a holiday."

"You don't know how I've dreamed about lying on the beach with you. Up at the NFD I'd play the tape of your voice and imagine we were together. I've been afraid that someone else would steal you away."

"No one has," I said.

"You still have school holidays, don't you? The ten days we were going to spend at the coast?"

When I nodded, he said, "This is just a thought—would you like to come back to the NFD with me? I'll understand if you say No. It's pretty primitive."

"But I'm saying Yes. I'd love to go." A chance to be with Ray AND see the far north of Kenya was too good to pass up. I'd been appalled when he showed me on the map where it was, right up against Ethiopia, but now I would go there. One beach was a lot like another beach, but the Northern Frontier was a world of its own.

"You're full of surprises," he said.

Joan finished her drink and came out. When we told her our plans, she looked stricken for a moment, and I felt I'd let her down. But she knew how I'd been looking forward to Ray's leave, and she and I had spent over two weeks together, longer than Ray and I would have had even with his leave. She recovered quickly and said, "I'll take the train to the coast tomorrow."

That night Joan said she had packing to do and stayed at my flat while Ray and I went to the Equator Club. I loved dancing with him, and I looked around to see if anybody I knew was there. I wanted to show him off. The only familiar face I saw was Tom Mboya's; the young politician and likely successor to Jomo Kenyatta was there with his fiancée.

Then Bilbander Gill waved from a nearby table and came across the floor towards us. I reached out to shake hands with him, and he took both my hands in his and we touched cheeks. "How are you, Emilee?" He glanced at Ray, who stood.

I introduced them. "Ray, Bill was very kind to me when I visited the tea plantation in Tanganyika."

The two men shook hands stiffly, then Bill said, "I'm visiting Mohan and I brought up a case of tea to ship to your parents."

I thought it had already been sent, but I thanked him profusely. "I haven't seen Mohan since before Christmas. Give my best wishes to him and Surgit," I said.

He smiled again and with a slight bow returned to his table. After he left, Ray said, "I didn't realize you knew any Asians." His tone said it was improper for a European woman to touch an Asian man in public.

"I've met the whole family," I said, "as well as the Puri family in Machakos. They've all been kind."

He said, "You make friends so easily. You have to be careful." He was more prophetic than he knew.

The next day while I packed and wrote a letter home, Ray visited with the Olivers, made phone calls and sent telegrams to arrange our trip. I could imagine the horrified officials who learned that an American woman would be accompanying Ray and two African constables to the NFD.

Early the following morning we were off to Nairobi, where he left his car for the Olivers and me to use while he was away, and picked up a police Land Rover that had a machine gun mounted on the roof and an *askari*, or African military escort, riding in back.

Our first stop was the Supermarket, where we loaded four shopping baskets with fresh food and staples to take with us. As we left Nairobi, another Land Rovers dropped in behind us. "Who's in that?" I asked.

"My cook and driver, and a couple more askaris. Plus lots of ammunition."

Having so many well-armed escorts made me feel safe, but closed-in too. "I'm looking forward to having time alone with you," I said.

Ray laughed lightly. "There are two other police officers living at the house," he said. "And haven't you noticed that there's nowhere in Kenya to be alone? There's always someone nearby, working and watching."

He was right. That was one reason I didn't want a fulltime servant.

I enjoyed seeing the Highlands again, the first time I'd passed that way since Surgit had brought me from Uganda.

We stopped for the night at Kitale. Ray made arrangements for the askaris' and his cook's food and lodging, then we went to our rooms. I'd just had a bath and gotten dressed for dinner when he tapped on my door and came in. My room was tiny, with only one chair, so we sat on the bed and kissed. Eventually I said, "We probably should go to the dining room before they stop serving."

"Umm," he murmured in that way the British have of indicating they've heard you and may even agree, but are taking no immediate action. Finally, though, we went to eat dinner, all six courses of it.

Later I was back in my room, truly alone. Lights went out all over the hotel and I lay awake for a while, smelling the fragrance of the eucalyptus trees that grew outside.

Ray was always well organized, so when we left the next morning we took picnic lunches he'd had the hotel prepare. "There's nowhere to eat on the way," he explained. "Or for any other needs." That meant no restrooms.

I was sorry I'd had so much tea for breakfast, but the desert air dehydrated me so that I sipped more tea and water from thermoses as we drove.

Kitale was the last semblance of a town. The road ahead was two faint tracks across the bush, and the only other vehicle was the one following us.

We passed the NFD road repair crew—a man leaning on a shovel—and a few miles farther on had to stop for a roadblock at a strategic point where the road went through a canyon. The roadblock was two metal poles embedded in the rocky earth with a longer pole crosswise between them. Ray signed the logbook registering that we were entering Turkana District, and lifted the pole. Both Land Rovers passed through, and an askari jumped off to replace the pole.

As we drove, breeze from the open windows whipped my hair into a dried tangle and I felt my khaki slacks sticking to my legs with perspiration. Ray looked as neat as he had at breakfast, and his starched shorts still had creases.

Just before lunch we passed a group of Turkana men, dressed only in their traditional short cape that hung down behind. "I hope it doesn't embarrass you to see a naked man," Ray said. I saw he was blushing slightly.

"I've seen a naked man before," I said. "I've been married."

He usually didn't talk while he was driving, but at that he turned slightly to me and said, "I'm relieved. I've been trying to figure out why someone like you wouldn't be married." Just what I'd wondered about him.

Late in the afternoon we reached Lodwar and parked beside the District Commissioner's house, a long whitewashed mansion that looked like something out of 'Arabian Nights.' Unlike the desert we'd driven through all day, the D. C.'s house was set in a lush garden. Bougainvillea tumbled in sprays of red and purple over stone walls, and papaya trees lifted their ruffled leaves like miniature palms.

Ray introduced me to the D.C., Geoffrey Hill, and took our bags to our rooms. "The bathroom's that way," he said. "You probably want to get rid of travel grime. And enjoy the luxury. Things will be different at Lokitaung."

After a bath I joined the men on the veranda. We weren't the only guests. The D. C.'s house was the 'hotel' for anyone traveling in the NFD, and he'd be reimbursed for expenses. A doctor up from Nairobi had been there several days, running a clinic to vaccinate the local people. Two Irish priests, looking like they'd stepped out of *Canterbury Tales*, sat drinking and chatting. I was the only woman.

The D. C. had dammed up the Turkwell River that flowed nearby, and had water pumped up to his house for household use and to irrigate the garden that grew vigorously just beyond the veranda. He even had watermelons and corn, two crops notorious for using a lot of water.

From the veranda we looked down on a group of round stone huts with cone-shaped roofs, and beyond, a volcanic mountain. "That's Lodwar Mountain," Ray explained, just as the sound of an airplane blotted out conversation. When it had passed over, he went on, "We're on the flight path from Europe to Nairobi. Pilots take a fix on the mountain. The huts are the prison compound where Jomo Kenyatta stayed for seven years."

Prison compound at Lodwar

"It must be minimum security," I said. "I don't see any barbed wire or fences."

"No need," the D.C. explained. "Anybody who escaped would die before he could walk to Kitale."

"It's lovely here," I said.

"Yes, I'll hate to leave it, but they don't want us staying too long in one place. Might go crazy like the poor bloke who went berserk when somebody killed his hunting spider. When I come back from leave I'll be posted somewhere else. I'll miss Lodwar, but I could do with a bit more civilization."

The D. C. had two refrigerators, one for food and the other for drinks, and both were used that evening. The next morning at breakfast I had papaya with lime and struggled with the thousand tiny bones of a kippered herring, which was too salty anyway for anyone driving across the desert.

We crossed a *lugga,* a vast expanse of white sand that Ray said turned into an impassable stream in the rain, and reached Lokitaung by noon. There were three European houses at Lokitaung, each on its own hill: one for the District Officer, one for the Police Superintendent and the third for the staff officer's house, where Ray lived. We drove up our hill, unloaded, and Ray's cook set to work preparing lunch.

Afterward, Ray suggested I might like to take a nap while he went over to the police post on business. I heard a Land Rover drive up and someone cursing. Then I heard Ray say, "Please watch your language. There's a lady resting in my house."

The other let out a string of expletives and roared off in the Land Rover.

Ray came in laughing and explained: "My apologies for the illiterate thug who is my boss. You aren't supposed to be here. Women aren't usually allowed in Lokitaung and civilians coming in during hostilities is forbidden."

"Oh, then you're in trouble. I'm sorry," I said, wondering if I'd have to leave immediately, and how.

"I took care of everything. Geoff Hill liked you, and gave me a letter addressed to Paddy giving express permission for you to be here. I'm sure Paddy is sending telegrams to everybody he can think of, trying to end my career. I'll give him a little longer before I show him the letter."

"You're enjoying this, aren't you?"

He laughed. "He'll make my life a living hell, but it will be worth it to see his face when he sees Geoff Hill's signature."

Ray Goodwin at Lokitaung Police Post, NFD of Kenya

The police house was bigger than my flat, but it was home to three men, and now me. Ray put my bag in his room and moved his things in with Tony. Edgar kept his own room.

"Water's scarce, so when you take a bath, don't pull the plug," Ray instructed. "I'll take a bath in the same water, and then we'll leave it in the tub to flush the toilet. Tomorrow night Tony and Edgar will have baths."

"Where does the water come from?"

"Camels bring it," Ray said.

That night I was startled awake by a clanging and bumping. I sat up in bed, tugged the mosquito net free and pulled on a robe. By that time, Ray was tapping on my door. "Would you like to see the camels?"

He led me to the porch and shone a torch (flashlight) on the camels, stamping impatiently while the heavy copper tanks they carried were lifted up to the water barrel on the roof and emptied. They snorted and shifted and finally shambled back down the hill, dark shapes in the starlight.

Ray's cohorts covered for him as much as possible while I was there so we could be together. One day he took me to the police station, a grand name for the hut with a porch where Africans waited to report cow theft, tribal movements and assaults.

An African approached, fortunately not naked in front. He wore a burlap loincloth and a huge feathered headdress. I grabbed my camera. "Ray, let me photograph you handling his complaint."

It took me a few seconds to set the shutter speed and focus. Ray muttered, "Hurry up! There's only so much we can say about this bit of paper." I got the photo.

I saw the walled enclosure, guarded by an askari, where dismantled weapons were kept. In the time it would take a trespasser to find the right parts to make up a weapon and assemble it, he would surely be discovered and arrested.

Another day we went to the duka, or general store, operated by an Indian. Turkana men, women and children crowded around, laughing and pointing at me. "Most of them have never seen a white woman before," Ray explained, "and they're laughing at how you're dressed." The men were naked, except for the tiny blanket hanging from their shoulders in back. Children, many ashen-faced from malnutrition, wore only leather loincloths. The women wore long skirts and lots of beads, leaving their breasts bare. I had on a long-sleeved blouse and Bermuda shorts, unnecessarily covering my breasts but leaving my legs immodestly bare, in their opinion.

On Sunday afternoon we drove north along Lake Rudolph to Todenyang, an abandoned mud-brick fortress that looked like something out of "Beau Geste." Built in the sand a good distance from the lake, the fortress had been flooded when the rains of two months before raised the lake level to historic highs. The walls had never been intended to withstand high water, and as the lake seeped into the core, the walls sagged and collapsed.

We swam in shallow water inside the fortress and were sunning ourselves on a warm rock when two fishermen paddled past and hailed us. They held up a huge fish they'd caught, and the bargaining began. After they and Ray agreed on a price, they posed for me, their skins glistening with water, the silver disks implanted in their chins glittering in the sunlight.

Two Fishermen at Lake Rudolph

We ate fish for the next three days. The second night a priest from a nearby mission came for dinner. "Why didn't Father Benjamin come?" Edgar asked.

"He doesn't drink, you know, and he was sure you police would be drinking."

"And right he was," Edgar agreed, pouring a round of gin for everybody.

After dinner I sat back and let the conversation flow around me while I knitted on Ray's sock. When I'd asked him what he wanted for his birthday in February, he said, "Knit me some socks." I knew how to knit, but I'd never made socks. I figured I could do it if I set my mind to it. Ray chose the yarn in Nairobi, and I was almost finished with the first sock.

Eventually the priest said he'd have to go. "Have another drink," Edgar urged. "You know Father Benjamin would want you to."

The priest shook his head. "No, there's no way of knowing what someone who doesn't drink would be thinking."

Word came that a British air force Beverley would be landing at Lodwar the next day bringing supplies. This would be a good way for me to get back to Nairobi without the grueling overland trip, so Tony agreed to drive me down to Lodwar. Ray had to make up the time the others had allowed him while I was there.

Tony and I set off right after breakfast, and when we got to Lodwar there was a telegram from Ray, saying how much he missed me already.

We watched the Beverley land, like a huge bumblebee with short stubby wings. It turned and rumbled back up the strip, stopped before the D. C., and the crew began to unload it. Then came the bad news: it had torn up the flood-ravaged dirt strip when it landed, and would have difficulty taking off. Only a sick African they were airlifting to a hospital would be taken on board, not me. Tony sent Ray a telegram telling him about the situation, we stayed overnight with the D.C. and drove down to Kitale the next day. The desk clerk handed me another loving telegram from Ray when I checked in. Tony enjoyed a night at Kitale before he had to turn back to Lokitaung. I took a bus to Nairobi and drove Ray's car to Machakos. My adventure was over. Another term began.

Chapter 11: Changes

By a fluke, I found myself Head of the Department of Education. The former Head had returned to the UK, and the only other person in the department was part time. Ergo, I was in charge. I knew nothing about what I was to teach as an education lecturer, and indeed very little about the British education system in general, only what I'd remembered from Makerere and observed since coming to Machakos. But I would learn.

The new responsibility brought no extra pay, but it meant I'd have a classroom of my own. My predecessor had been artistic and had left behind several good posters. One that I kept on display for months showed a wide-eyed African child saying, "Ooh, that looks interesting. Can I try?" I thought that was the attitude good teachers tried to attain.

I inherited a cupboard that contained a few more posters and a chewed-up copy of the *Historical Survey on the Origin and Growth of Mau Mau*, known locally as the Corfield Report.

Part of my job was to issue, collect and account for textbooks. I thought I could handle that with no trouble, but I discovered that the books had no individual numbers, so there was no way to prove which student had been issued which book. At the end of term missing books were debited to everybody's deposit, so that even if a student had not lost a book, she ended up losing a portion of the cost of one. The college seemed to think this system was easier to administer than assessing individual fines. It pushed conscientious students to locate and turn in books wherever they found them. However, it encouraged dishonest students to hold on to books, knowing they would have to pay only a portion of the lost charge. The book distribution system to me marked a fundamental difference in culture between America and Africa. We believe in individual responsibility, whereas in tribal Africa, everybody works for the group and if necessary, suffers with the group.

That term I taught eight classes of education which each met twice weekly, and one English class, which met four times a week. Miss Thomas was still meeting my classes once a week for speech training. My own speech had taken on a few British intonations, but not enough for me to be trusted with future African speech.

I dug into the material I was supposed to teach my students: the best site for a school, what materials to use, where to locate latrines, and how to build a simple structure that could later be expanded easily and could even have glass installed in the window openings.

I felt comfortable teaching record keeping, class control and questioning techniques. I thought class control was an unnecessary topic, since I'd never seen any discipline problems in African schools, but I taught it anyway.

There were changes in my living arrangements too. Now that John was in jail, Muyia became my house servant as well as gardener. I paid him full wages and sometimes gave him an extra loaf of bread or bottle of milk. From the beginning he'd asked for empty jars and tins and old newspapers. The tins he used for small coffee plants or as drinking cups, and may have used the newspapers for mulch. Very little was wasted in Kenya.

My colleagues told me not to reward a servant with extra money. He'd only spend it on beer, they said, whereas extra food would be taken home to his family. I didn't think Muyia would deprive his family to drink beer, but I assumed the British teachers knew what was what.

One of the TEA teachers later told me of her experience trying to change the British system of treating servants. She asked her house servant how much he was paid. He told her. In her liberal American mindset, she wanted to change his life. "I'm cutting your hours in half, paying you twice what you've been earning, and I'm going to teach you English," she announced. The servant stared at her, puzzled and perhaps frightened. Surely she must be crazy. When he left that evening, she never saw him again and later learned he'd gone back to work for a British employer. He knew what to expect there.

Muyia kept the floors polished, did the laundry (all but women's panties, which Africans refused to touch and which thus were my responsibility) and washed up pots and pans, often in cold water. I always boiled water and scalded them after he'd left, though the longtime British teachers thought I was a bit of a zealot about germs.

One day when I had lunch with Margaret Lloyd, she had strawberries with cream for dessert. As I spooned mine up, I saw bits of hull sticking to the berries, and several bad spots.

She noticed and said, "I'll bet you're going to write your mother about these unsanitary berries. Well, you just write her that Miss Lloyd has been out here thirteen years eating things like this, and she's never been sick."

My garden was coming along merrily. The watermelon vines had three melons, each as big as a gallon bucket, the okra had formed pods that were almost ready to harvest, the string beans had put runners along the wire that separated my garden from the storm drain, and my lettuce was the wonder of the campus. I shared it with everybody and enjoyed it myself. It was clean and didn't have to be washed in potassium permanganate, a purple liquid used to disinfect suspicious vegetables.

Salesmen of various kinds showed up at lunchtime, selling carvings, paintings, lemons, vegetables and strawberries. The berries I bought were delicious, and I decided to grow some of my own. In Swahili I told the seller that I wanted plants, and a few days later he showed up with 35 good plants, wrapped in cornhusks. I gladly paid the 20 shillings he asked ($1.80) and had Muyia gather some cow manure from the pasture outside. He'd no sooner set the plants in where I indicated than it began to rain, so they lived and grew. Unknown to me, he'd already planted green peas there—I never knew where he got the seeds—so peas began to come up among the strawberries.

Ray had left his car for us, and while I didn't strip the gears as Chad did, it took a bit of practice to get used to shifting with my left hand in a pattern of four forward speeds, driving on the left and signaling with my right hand. As long as I kept straight ahead I was okay, but I had trouble with right turns. The first time I attempted one, I cut off another driver. Left turns were the easy ones in Kenya.

Ray had been meticulous about writing down the mileage at the beginning of each car trip, the date and destination. Beje, Chad and I were very lax about recording trips, which ruined Ray's logbook.

Back home, W-2 forms were being sent out ready for the filing of U. S. taxes for 1961. Part of the incentive to work in East Africa was being exempt from American taxes if we lived outside the States for 510 days in eighteen months. We paid East African taxes, which were lower than American, but had to file for an American extension until the eighteen months had passed. I wrote to the Computation Center at UNC where

I'd worked for W-2 forms, and to the State of North Carolina and the IRS for exemption forms.

In Nairobi I bought a silver-plated tea and coffee set that had belonged to a European family who had 'gone home.' Serving coffee and tea elegantly was a pleasant daily ritual in Kenya.

Many of my colleagues had spent years teaching in Kenya, and their flats showed it. They'd bought upholstered sofas and chairs to replace the government-issued wooden ones, Scandinavian dishes, Rowland-Ward crystal glassware, and Oriental carpets. My flat looked bare in comparison, but I was temporary. I always knew I'd return to America at the end of my two-year term. Still, I began to accumulate nice things, and to entertain more.

I was seeing a lot of Rico. Ray and I exchanged long weekly letters and made plans for Easter vacation together, but he was away, and Rico was there. Rico took me out about once a week, to the club or to the lake water skiing or into Nairobi for a movie or dancing. As we rode, he'd sing to me in Italian, or teach me a few words of the language, and I had bought a 'Teach Yourself Italian' book along with my 'Teach Yourself Swahili,' thinking that this was a good opportunity to learn a language, being around native speakers.

I told Rico I had been married in college and divorced, and was in love with Ray. He said, "Why are you telling me this? We are just having fun together, the two of us."

He was lonely. Ray had his police colleagues for company and I had the teachers and the Olivers. Rico supervised Africans, but didn't fraternize with them after work. Mario and Enrico were like family to him, but they were older, and didn't go dancing. I did.

He went for a holiday on the coast, so I didn't see him for several weeks. One day on the way back from Nairobi I went by his house. His houseboy let me in, murmured something plaintive in Swahili about the Bwana, and pointed toward the bedroom. I couldn't make out what he said over the sound of Enrico Caruso's singing; Rico had a set of very old Caruso records.

I tapped on the bedroom door and said "Hodi?"

"Emilee! Cara mia, come in!" He lay on the bed. "So, you have finally noticed that Rico is missing. I have been here sick with malaria for over a week, and nobody has come to check up on me. Come here and kiss me."

"But you're sick," I protested.

"You get malaria from mosquitoes, not from kissing Italians."

I laughed and kissed him.

Sometimes Rico would show up unannounced with flowers and food—and always a bottle of wine—and say, "Why don't we cook dinner? I was alone at my house and I thought, 'Emilee must be eating alone too, so why not join her?'" Once he brought a live lobster, and we managed to cook and eat it, though the scream it made when we plunged it into boiling water haunts me.

I felt disloyal to Ray spending time with Rico. When I told Beje Oliver how I felt, she asked, "Has Ray proposed?"

"No."

"He can't object to your seeing someone else if he's not committed to you. Besides, we want you to come to Texas when you leave Kenya and meet Jim, Chad's best friend. Chad and I both think you and Jim would be perfect together."

I knew Ray wasn't seeing anybody else. There was no woman to date within three hundred miles of him.

With Ray I felt safe and contented. He arranged things ahead of time and was very deliberate and reserved. With Rico I never knew what to expect. He was funny, spontaneous and complimentary. One night he came in and held out both hands in front of him, wrists together. "You have tamed the big lion. Why don't you tie me up and keep me here? I'll work for you for ten bob and posho," he concluded, using the common expression in Kenya for a servant's wages plus an allotment of cornmeal.

I just laughed and said I didn't need another houseboy.

Rico, Ray and I all had February birthdays, which would have made me discount astrological signs, if I'd ever put any stock in them. They were as different as two Caucasian men of the same age could be, in background, personality, and everything. While Ray as a child had endured wartime bombing and I was buying savings stamps and searching the farm for bits of discarded iron, Rico was a little con man, selling items on the black market. I'd attended a small rural school on the corner of our farm, Ray went to a boarding school, and Rico studied with priests.

Rico's birthday was first, which we celebrated with a bottle of champagne. Mine was Valentine's Day, and Ray's was the day after, as was Jim's, the Olivers' friend. I finished Ray's socks and got them off in time for his birthday. Beje made a poster that said 'Happy Birthday' followed by a paper heart and a space. First we lettered 'Ray' on a piece of paper, taped it to the poster and the two of us held it up while Chad took a Polaroid picture of it to send Ray. Then Beje took off the paper with Ray's name and stuck on one that said 'Jim,' and we held it while Chad took another photo. This, in addition to making a personalized birthday card, was their sneaky way to introduce me to Jim. Sure enough, in a couple of weeks they had a letter that began, "Dear Beje, Chad, Kim and Emilee."

On my birthday Beje and Kim gave me silver sugar tongs. I had cards from friends and family, and Rico took me to the East African premiere of "Spartacus." Kirk Douglas, the star, was there in person, looking much smaller than on screen. Rico also brought a box of chocolates that I shared in the teachers' lounge the next day.

Ray, however, made the dramatic birthday gesture. Puri's delivered a telegram from him at mid-morning, and about an hour later, roses. The truck pulled up at my house and the deliveryman almost staggered as he brought in eight dozen red roses! Puri must have raided all the Indian gardens in Machakos, for only a few were the typical florist-type long stemmed beauties. The others were in various shades of red, some wide open, some buds, some single flowered blossoms. I didn't have vases for half the roses, so I shared with the other teachers. Ray definitely knew how to make an impression, on me and the whole faculty.

But Ray as a memory couldn't compete with Rico's presence, and it wasn't his fault.

Ray called me one Saturday in early March from Kitale. I had just washed my hair and put on my bathing suit to go outside and tan while my hair dried. Miss Shrubsole's servant came to inform me of the call, and averted his eyes as he saw me outside indecently dressed. I wrapped a towel around my hair and ran over to her house, but by the time I got there the phone connection was broken. I sat and waited while the operator got Ray on the line and called me back.

"It's so good to hear your voice," he said. "I'm afraid that's all I can manage, though. I won't be able to make it to Machakos. I came down from the NFD this morning with a Turkana body for a post-mortem."

"Are you staying there overnight?"

"Yes. Can you drive up and stay over with me?"

"Oh! I'm on duty!" I moaned.

"I was afraid it would be something like that. I do miss you. Darling, say something."

What could I say? Miss Shrubsole was sitting nearby hearing everything. I should have said, "I love you," but I didn't, and he didn't. He said, "I miss you, and I can't wait for my next leave."

"Me too," I said, and then, unsatisfactorily, we said good-bye.

In retrospect, I should have run around the campus until I found a teacher who would pull duty for me, then driven the five hours to Kitale to be with Ray. With any luck, I could have just made it before dark, and we would have had an evening and night together. But I didn't, and a chance for us to be together was lost. That might have changed everything.

Chapter 12: Multiracial Kenya

Kenya delegates were meeting in London with representatives of Her Majesty's Government to decide Kenya's future. Tanganyika had become independent, with Julius Nyerere as its president. It had been German East Africa, so the British didn't have a strong sense of ownership of that territory. Uganda's independence was slated for October, and everybody expected it to go smoothly as a constitutional monarchy. King Freddie, the Kabaka of Uganda, would retain his throne, and Milton Obote was the likely president. It was a prosperous, multiracial country, but relatively few Europeans had settled in Uganda.

Kenya was different. Called 'the country club of the British Empire,' it was home to many Europeans, some of them third generation Kenyans. They liked the climate, the beauty of the country, and the lifestyle. They were loath to give all that up, especially to turn the reins of government over to Jomo Kenyatta, a hero to the Africans but a traitor to the British. After studying in the UK and marrying a British woman, he had come back to lead Mau Mau, a group that in the name of independence had murdered Africans as well as Europeans in the 1950's. Seven years of detention had mellowed him, but could Europeans trust him?

Not knowing what *uhuru* might bring, people speculated about the future. Should they sell out and leave? Teachers and others on contract pondered what would be the best time to retire, based on their years of employment versus years left to work. Should they take a lump sum or a pension spread out over decades?

Men in the various British services had another consideration. They paid a portion of their salaries into a fund for widows and orphans. If they were still single when they quit the service—and thus had no wives or children who could become widows and orphans—their payments were refunded. For this reason, many a man postponed marriage until after he had received and deposited his refund.

Ray was a practical, orderly man and would undoubtedly want a refund. He'd mentioned staying on in Kenya after uhuru and perhaps finding a private job.

Suppose uhuru came suddenly, before my contract ended? Would I stay on and see what happened, or should I be ready to leave hurriedly, never mind the tax consequences? Some people talked vindictively of destroying whatever they owned if they were forced out, so no Africans could benefit from their property. I had no such feelings, for I'd had only pleasant experiences in Africa, and I owned very little there anyway. It was the uncertainty that kept people on edge and made planning difficult.

Kenya was changing, if not in attitude then certainly in outward signs. In late February the Machakos Club voted to become multi-racial. They didn't expect a great influx of Asian or African members, and guests had to be approved by six of the fifteen committee members. And Americans of whatever race were classified European. Still, it was a start.

It was done primarily because of Rufus, the American Negro (as he was referred to then) on our project assigned to Machakos Boys Secondary School. He was no more an African than I, but because of his skin color, only the African Club had been available to him. We were both Americans, and in interacting in Kenya, we began to realize how very

American we were. We had more in common with each other than Rufus had with Africans or I with Europeans.

That realization should have been a 'Heads up' to me about my relationships with Ray and Rico, but I ignored it.

New club members had to be approved by all fifteen committee members. I agreed to be the House Member, which meant I was responsible for arranging social events and checking on the dishes, linens and so on for the club. It was a mistake. I did a poor job and eventually resigned, but not until I'd cast my vote to accept Rufus as a member.

As part of preparing our students for the future, not just as teachers but as citizens, we took them on field trips to Nairobi to see their Legislative Council (called Legco) and courts in action, and to observe a multiracial school. We had lunch at City Park, allowed the girls an hour or so for shopping, and then headed back to college.

Downtown Nairobi

Our students already had some idea of racial blending, for they came from fourteen tribes. At Machakos, they got along with each other, and all communicated in English.

If a small group went on a trip, we squeezed into a van. For large groups, a lorry outfitted with seats in the back was used. We parked in the municipal lot and walked first to Legco.

Legco was (and is) a beautiful building. The main room, paneled in walnut, had leather-covered seats. The speaker, wearing a black robe and a white curly wig, sat in a leather-covered chair before a huge British Coat-of-Arms. Tom Mboya, whom the American press referred to as 'silver-tongued,' was speaking one day when I took a group, and the description fitted him. He made a good impression in Kenya and abroad, and was a rival to Kenyatta. His career was somewhat limited, however, as he belonged to the Luo, one of the smaller tribes, and not the powerful Kikuyu.

The behavior of the Legco members seemed rude. They walked around, ate, and drank while someone was speaking, and hammered or kicked their desks to show disagreement.

Outside, on the way back to the college bus, we passed the American Consulate, and the sight of our flag fluttering in Nairobi gave me mixed feelings: pride, homesickness, and relief that I had a country I could go back to after uhuru.

Few of our students were likely to teach in a school as well appointed as the multi-racial school we visited later. It drew from the upper classes, and the student body were mostly Asian, with a sprinkling of Europeans and Africans. Their classrooms were well equipped and their uniforms neat and complete, down to white socks and well-polished shoes. They all learned in English, the language of Kenya's future, and they got on well together. That was the point.

City Park, where we went for a picnic lunch, was a pleasant surprise: several hundred acres of well-cared-for flowers and shrubs, including huge beds of exotic blue and orange Bird of Paradise. We ate sitting on the grass beside a gurgling brook. Another surprise was in store afterward, not so pleasant: my first Asian toilet. In my travels I was later to see many more of these hole-in-the-floor toilets, but I hadn't expected them in Nairobi.

While my students shopped, I made my weekly wonderful visit to the Municipal Market. I tried to avoid the meat section, which never smelled good enough to entice me to buy, and went instead to the fruit, vegetable and flower stalls. For $1.60 on one of these visits I bought a head of lettuce, two pounds of tomatoes, a pineapple, six tangerines, three oranges, two grapefruit, a dozen bananas, a bunch of sweet peas and two dozen carnations. Kenya was a cornucopia of produce.

Later the students and I went to a school for the blind where children studied Braille, their fingertips feeling quickly for the raised markings that could give them information. They were eager to talk to us, exploring our faces with their hands, frowning and saying "Aieeh!" when they discovered that my features felt different, not African. Many of Kenya's blind were also albinos, eerie-looking outcasts from their society. Their colorless, almost translucent skin and pale eyes that focused on nothing gave them an alien, otherworldly quality. They were the most eager of all students for attention and affection, and most afraid to seek it. They shyly put out their hands, seeking ours.

I left feeling disturbed. After independence the members of Legco, driving Mercedes cars and wearing Saville Row suits, would flourish. So too would the privileged children at the multi-racial school. But what would happen to the poor unfortunates at the school for the blind, and the lepers we always saw sitting begging on the sidewalk beside Government

Road? Who would care for them?

Soon after, a thoroughly British multi-racial event took place in Machakos: the Duke and Duchess of Gloucester made a royal visit to Kenya, where he reviewed the King's African Rifles, whom he'd commanded in World War II. The Duke was the uncle of Queen Elizabeth, and the Duchess, called Lady Alice, was known to many Kenyans.

The Machakos teachers were excited about the visit and got dressed up in silk suits and hats and went down to the parade ground. I didn't own a hat, and wore my usual skirt and blouse outfit, but the event didn't involve me anyway.

The Duchess, resplendent in a bright pink suit, hat and matching shoes, and the Duke in khaki uniform, went down the line shaking hands with the Machakos district dignitaries and then with the remnants of the KAR. The African veterans brought a lump to my throat, and I wasn't British or Kenyan. Each man wore what he had left of his uniform: a hat, a coat, a baton, or medals pinned onto his shabby shirt. Some limped, and others had shirtsleeves pinned up to cover the stump where an arm had been.

Each man bowed before the Duchess and saluted the Duke. Then the active KAR marched out, the band wearing leopard skins across their chests and bright topis on their heads, their instruments glittering in the sunlight. I grabbed my camera and ducked under the rope that separated the spectators from the performers. A group of men were there taking photos and didn't mind my joining them. I discovered later that they were the press and I had broken an unwritten rule about getting too close to royalty. I had embarrassed Miss Shrubsole, who had already told me some locals were referring to me as the 'dreadful American' because I'd been seen holding hands with Rico at the lake. But I got some colorful photos.

The Duchess of Gloucester greets the King's African Rifles (Alison Shrubsole at right)

One Sunday Rico took me to the cement company's field day, another multi-racial event. I sat in the stands amid African women with babies tied to their backs, Asians in saris and a sprinkling of European wives. Rico competed in everything, but only won the discus throw and shot putt. He was too heavy and muscular—and at thirty too old—for pole vaulting or running. Young African workers won all those competitions.

I continued to be fascinated with Africa, and blithely ignored racial and cultural barriers. Margaret Lloyd, a Welsh teacher at the college, felt as I did, and that formed the original basis for our friendship, for we differed on many other issues.

Traces of racial prejudice showed up in strange, subtle ways. It had been nearly a year since I last saw a dentist, so I located one in Nairobi and made an appointment with him. "He's an Ismaili," one of the British teachers protested.

His religion made no difference to me. I only cared about his ability to clean teeth and fill cavities. As far as I could tell, he did good work. I was satisfied to pay the $7 he charged for cleaning my teeth and filling one cavity. And he was definitely an Ismaili. A huge signed photo of the young Karim, Aga Khan, hung in his office, looking right at me as I sat in the dental chair. I told the dentist I admired the American-educated Karim, who had taken responsibility as religious leader in his twenties.

He smiled proudly, and told me about entertaining Aly Khan and Rita Hayworth when they'd visited the Ismaili community in Kenya. He said he'd try to introduce me to the Aga Khan the next time the leader came to Kenya, but it never happened.

I continued to see Mohan, inviting him out to the college to have dinner, along with Margaret and the Olivers. He invited me into Nairobi for films, lunch and once to see barracks his company had just completed.

"We're looking to some other country, maybe Iran," he said. "My father came to Africa in 1927 with nothing, and now we're millionaires, but it could all be taken away by an African government. We're disbanding the construction company, but there's nothing we can do about the tea plantation."

"I loved visiting there," I said. "I hate to think of it being broken up into little shambas."

He nodded. "We have to face facts. I enjoy being rich, but I could always go somewhere and start over with nothing if I had to."

I never had another blatantly prejudiced experience like my first evening in Nairobi with Surgit. Meeting Mohan at The Thorn Tree didn't bother me. He'd approach, smiling and handsome, and if anybody took note of us and was bothered, it was their problem, not mine.

Nairobi, like most of East Africa, was multi-racial biologically if not legally, and always had been. To me, it was the most exciting place on earth to be right then. London, Paris and New York were old cities, but Nairobi was young as cities go, and it was where things were happening. Multi-racial things.

Chapter 13: Duty and Decisions

Easter was approaching, and the end of my second term in Kenya.

On April 8, I had Sunday duty, and I seemed to be a jinx as far as duty was concerned.

Church services were held in the dining hall as soon as breakfast was cleared away. It was Anglican so I went over to attend, but just as the Holy Communion portion of the service began, a busload of male students from Kitui arrived to visit with our girls.

"Visiting hours begin at two," I told their chaperone firmly, and sent them away to the boys' school for lunch. "Come back then."

As I got back to the door of the dining hall, a girl staggered out of the church service and fainted at my feet. She didn't have malaria symptoms of chills and fever, so I took a long chance that she had nothing serious and got her back to the dorm to bed, gave her aspirin, and crossed my fingers.

By then it was time to open the dispensary. Six girls showed up with a rash from an insect called 'Nairobi Eye,' which spits out an acid-like substance that burns the skin.

Afterward, I supervised the weighing-out of food for the rest of the day's meals, welcomed back the busload of visiting boys, greeted the other guests, and eventually saw all the visitors off, locked the office and took evening roll call.

One group was missing—a busload of girls who had gone into Nairobi. They arrived back about nine, and had to be given dinner. Finally at ten I made my rounds and announced lights out. No other duty day was ever as bad as Sunday.

On Friday night before term break the students presented an amusing set of one-act plays. I was technically supervising, but the students themselves had chosen the plays, cast and directed them, and improvised wildly on costumes and props. In one play, set in 19th century Russia, a military officer walked in wearing an army surplus poplin windbreaker, a teacher's borrowed plaid slacks and my black rubber rain boots. For an action scene, the girls used long-handled scrub brushes for muskets and pangas for swords, the latter almost too realistically dangerous. Their transposing of *l* and *r* brought laughs where none were intended; for example, one line was "I have rearned my resson about rove." Translation: "I have learned my lesson about love."

The following day was Old Students' Day, an unflattering term to describe alumni. Since I hadn't been at Machakos long enough for any of the 'old' students to come by and reminisce with me, I slipped away early.

Rico was helping me study Swahili—he had an ear for languages, and even sang operas in Swahili, transposing them easily from Italian—and I helped him with his English. He was planning to take an exam in English that might mean a promotion and study that would lead to a chemical engineering degree, so we spent a lot of time together.

He took me to tour the cement plant. He led me past piles of limestone and gypsum, across metal catwalks above giant crushers and huge vats of slurry kept in motion by a paddle wheel. He pointed out the vast cooker that turned the mixture into cement, indicated the dials and valves. Part of his job was to make sure nothing exploded, and after the cooking, to supervise cleaning the tank.

On Monday and Tuesday the students packed, and cleaned the classrooms and dormitories. The next morning we inspected the dorms, pronounced them satisfactorily clean, and checked off students as they boarded buses at 7:30 to go home on holidays. Two were to stay on campus the entire time. They were emotionally disturbed, and Miss Shrubsole thought they would be better off at Machakos.

We'd been told that Africans were having to cover a thousand years of learning and progress in fifty years or less, and for some of our students, the stress was too much. In any culture, children returning home from college bring back disturbing changes, but in Kenya in the 1960's the difference was like the great split in the earth that had produced the Escarpment—two sections of earth lay on different levels, and it was difficult to get from one to the other.

Occasionally I'd see an African woman trudging across the pasture behind her husband, a strap digging into her scalp to balance a heavy load that bent her double. He strode ahead, tapping the ground with a walking stick. Her hands would be busy weaving a basket as she walked.

How would our students adjust to their home world, to mothers and sisters like this, when they'd seen their teachers living independently, driving cars, handling their own money? No wonder some were emotionally disturbed.

I was feeling disturbed myself. I was falling in love with Rico, and he urged me to marry him. He was always very emotional and persuasive, and I said yes.

But what about Ray? His long-postponed leave was looming, and with it our trip to the coast. I was torn between two men, and I couldn't have them both. I could have gone with Ray, hoping he wouldn't find out about Rico, but I was always brutally honest, even when it was not in my best interests to be so.

Rico said, "When you see your British gentleman again, you will forget all about me."

"No, I won't." I chose him, but to make sure I didn't see Ray and waver in my decision, I took the coward's way out.

Ray was planning to meet Chad, Beje and me for lunch at The Lobster Pot in Nairobi, then come out to Machakos afterward to spend the night before we left for the coast. I wrote him a letter saying I couldn't go with him, that I planned to marry Rico, and gave it to Beje. I stayed away from Nairobi that day.

Beje told me later that Ray was late arriving and she and Chad discussed what they'd say and do if he reacted badly. They knew what my letter contained. But when he read it, he froze, and after a few minutes said, "Excuse me, I have to make a phone call." It wasn't to me.

If he'd called, or driven straight to my flat and said, 'you can't marry him. I love you,' I would have gone with him anywhere. But he didn't.

I tried later to tell him how wrong I had been. But there are things in life that can't be changed by saying, 'I'm sorry. I made a mistake.' This was one of them.

Chapter 14: Easter Holidays

The next day Beje invited me for lunch—with Ray. He had ordered a curry luncheon delivered to her house and wanted me to join them. He'd planned it from the Frontier.

Common sense told me to refuse, but I went. I scarcely tasted the curry, usually my favorite meal, and conversation was strained. Sitting across the table from him was torture. We looked at each other mutely while Beje and Kim chatted. What if I had told him then I was giving up Rico, and asked for another chance? He probably would have rejected me, I thought, so I said nothing.

He gave us the address of his new posting and left.

Rico went out of his way during the next week to keep me busy. We shopped in Nairobi, poking among curio shops full of drums, monkey skin rugs, baskets and woven reed tablemats, and Indian tables inlaid with mosaics. We had dinner at the Swiss Grill and attended the opera, "Lucia de Lamermoor"—performed by puppets. As the puppet depicting the mad Lucia swayed across the miniature stage, the recorded voice of Beverly Sills filled the room, and Rico whispered translations for me.

On Saturday we joined thousands of others to watch the East African Safari, the world's most grueling road race. No zooming round and round a paved, banked track here. The 3,600-mile route crossed the deserts of Kenya and Tanganyika, skirted Lake Victoria in Uganda, forded streams and bumped over rutted rocky trails. Some cars became airborne cresting a hill at 60 mph or rounding a blind curve. The race went on day and night until the last car arrived at the finish line or was disabled and dropped out. The Safari attracted world champion drivers, including Britain's Sterling Moss, driving a Saab, and Kenya's challenger, Jagander Singh in a Mercedes.

Rico and I watched at one of the checkpoints, on the Athi River-Magadi Road. Drivers swerved in, got their names checked off, their mileage registered to make sure they had followed the route, made a pit stop, and were off in a cloud of dust. To keep from blinding each other with dust, the cars left at three-minute intervals. We never saw two cars racing bonnet to bonnet (what the British called the 'hood') so it wasn't very exciting. It was an endurance test. Winning was a combination of driving time plus the condition of the car when it was inspected at the end of the race.

The following day, Easter Sunday, we headed up-country to an Italian house party in Nakuru. Our hosts, a family of four, had five other guests in addition to us, and over the weekend we consumed vast quantities of food and six gallons of wine! Surely neighbors who dropped in were responsible for a lot of it. One of these was a much-married multi-lingual woman. She'd married an Italian, a Frenchman and an Englishman, and spoke seven languages.

On Easter Monday Joe, our host, took Rico and me to visit several Highlands farms. Mau Mau had been especially bad there, and ownership of this land was causing trouble in deciding who'd own it after uhuru.

The first farm spread over 65,000 acres, and the owner had created a world of baronial splendor, including her own Gothic style church with stained glass windows. Housing for her African workers covered a hillside.

The altitude there was nearly 10,000 feet, so the days were always cool. At the next farm, a family lounged in sweaters and slacks by a fire in a fireplace four feet by seven. The children were brought in by their African *ayah* to meet us, and a servant in a long *kunzu* padded in quietly with a tray of coffee, hot milk and cake. The host and hostess invited us to come back for a weekend or a week. They were isolated, they said, and enjoyed having visitors.

The third place was the most beautiful: a gray stone mansion with picture windows facing a lawn like green velvet and a garden lush with flowers of all seasons blooming at once: daffodils, calla lilies, irises, roses, carnations, winter honeysuckle, snapdragons and chrysanthemums.

Such beauty and luxury those people had! I could understand why they loved Kenya and why they would fight to keep it intact. And yet, I didn't envy them more than a few moments. The timeless days and loneliness were not for me. I was glad to have a job I enjoyed and colleagues to talk to. I missed libraries and having my own telephone, but Machakos was a good place to be.

I returned to my flat determined to make more of what I had there. I went on a cleaning binge, rearranging furniture and sorting out closets.

My garden was flourishing. My first watermelon had been destroyed by worms, but my second seemed perfect, and was almost ripe. My strawberries were blooming, producing ripe berries and putting out runners. Gardening in Kenya meant forgetting about seasons as I knew them and instead planting with the rains.

In the next few days Muyia and I planted chrysanthemums, tuberoses, marigolds, carnations, verbena, petunias, peppers, broccoli, radish and lettuce, all crowded together. These were for me, to be enjoyed soon. For the future, for whoever would live in my flat, I ordered eight rose bushes.

One morning when I looked out the kitchen window I thought the earth had cracked open, leaving a foot-wide chasm. Instead, it was safari ants, a mass of millions of the giant insects that crawled inexorably across the campus, eating their way then across the pasture and on toward the club. My flat was right in their path.

They reached me, devouring the geraniums by my back door. Then the column split, half crawling along the ground, the other half going up the door facing, across the top and down the other side to join the main column once more. Muyia boiled water and poured on them. I gave him a container of insecticide I'd purchased to kill cockroaches under the sink, and he sprinkled it about cheerfully. He came in to report, "Wote kwenda." ("They are all going.") They were, but they would have gone anyway, regardless of our puny efforts. We'd killed a few thousand, but the mass never noticed. They were as heedless of humans as they'd been for eons. I was relieved they hadn't come inside the house.

During school holidays I had more time to study languages and to read. I reread Robert Ruark's *Something of Value*, about Mau Mau. It made a lot more sense to me, having seen the area where it all took place, and it seemed sadder too, for I could sympathize with the Africans' frustration and the Europeans' love of Kenya and fear of losing what they'd worked for. There was no happy ending in Ruark's book, and there would probably be none for many Kenyans of all races.

Ruark himself was staying in Nairobi, researching his next book, *Uhuru*. *The East African Standard* interviewed him about his writing and he described his life at Chapel Hill. I wanted to go visit him and say, "I attended Carolina. I'm a Tarheel too," but the reporter protected Ruark's privacy by not revealing where he was staying, and I never saw him at The Thorn Tree. A later news article told of Ruark's being mauled by a leopard in one of the game parks. He flew home to America to recuperate and finish his book.

I was still writing home asking my mother to get me tax forms for Virginia, North Carolina and the U. S. Government, and copies of my W-2 forms from North Carolina. I had until June 15 to file. The original forms had been sent sea mail and hadn't arrived. I had holidays and a servant, while Mama was teaching, doing her own housework and freezing strawberries back home, but she managed to send me all the papers on time.

Beje and Chad were counting down the weeks, then the days, until they left for America, and we often fantasized about what we'd do and eat when we got home. Beje planned to cook and eat five pounds of good bacon, even if she got sick as a result. The British bacon was something like what we called a picnic ham, a big lump of meat to be boiled. Their ham they called gammon, and when it was fried for breakfast, the fatty portion was limp and translucent. We dreamed of crisp, salty, thin-sliced American bacon. I also wanted sausages that were seasoned with sage instead of cinnamon, and pancakes served with real maple syrup, not the British treacle (molasses) or 'golden syrup,' which was sweet but flavorless.

Chad planned to watch the University of Texas play football. Soccer and rugby didn't fill the bill for him, and none of us ever managed to sit through an entire cricket match, which seemed to go on for days.

One night in early May two unexpected visitors arrived about seven-thirty, Kay Strain and Pat McGowan, two of my favorites on the TEA project. They had both just received their master of education degrees from Makerere, and would now have two years of teaching in Kenya.

Kay was assigned to teach at the girls' secondary school in the hill above Machakos, so I now had three Americans nearby, in addition to the Olivers. I invited Kay and Pat to have supper and spend the night, which they had been counting on, while I frantically considered what to serve.

Beje came to my rescue with a pan of lasagna.

The next day Pat went to his posting at Nyeri, northeast of Nairobi, and I took Kay into Nairobi to register at the U. S. Consulate and at Kenya Immigration, and to buy things to furnish her flat.

I knew the drill, for I was now the veteran.

Chapter 15: Opportunities and Difficulties

School started again in mid-May and I faced another complex schedule. I was to teach five more classes each week than I had the previous term, and all my teaching days began at 7:30 a.m. In addition, I had to make out exams for six classes and, as Education Head, arrange the schedule for demonstration lessons on Wednesdays for five weeks.

Since I had the power to schedule, I only scheduled myself for two demonstration lessons, leaving me three free Wednesdays.

In demonstration lessons lecturers taught what was supposed to be a model lesson, so the first-year students could see how it should be done. Some MTC lecturers were very clever at using local materials in teaching. For example, Cecily Nevill used beans and maize seeds to teach counting and subtracting, and Miss Anderson took slides of local features and animals for her geography classes. The art teacher improvised materials by using various shades of clay for paint, and made brushes from well-chewed twigs.

First Years observed for two days, came back to college for five days of preparation (making maps, charts, lesson plans, etc.) and returned to the schools for three weeks of practice teaching. Meanwhile, the Second Years had two days of review, five days of study and two days of exams.

Student Teaching

They would then have regular classes, but on a different schedule, until the end of the First Years' teaching practice. In July everybody would go onto a 'normal' schedule. I wondered how the students knew when to go where. I couldn't remember and consulted my schedule every night to know what I'd do at 7:30 a.m.

May was the time for the 'long rains,' which lived up to their name. The new bridge over the Athi River had only been opened to traffic for two weeks, and already floodwater was rising toward the floor of it. We kept our fingers crossed that the soft dirt at both ends would hold and we'd be able to go to Nairobi when we wanted to.

Ray was still posted away and had left his car with the Olivers, who let me use it, although Ray stipulated—fairly enough—that I was not to use it to go to see Rico.

I drove it one rainy day to Mumbuni School to arrange for observation. The driveway into the school was so muddy that I worried about getting stuck and left Ray's car parked beside of the road, about a thousand yards from the school. When I came back fifteen minutes later, someone had stolen the side mirror. The chrome arm that held it was still there, but was twisted where the thief had wrung the mirror out of its socket.

Another day when the student teacher and I went into the classroom where she was to teach, the pupils were all seated, but there was no teacher's desk, only a chair. "Where is the teacher's desk?" she asked.

The class answered in unison, "It was stolen."

I couldn't imagine why anyone would steal a rickety wooden table, unless for firewood, but such things were happening with more frequency. Some government tax officials set up tables and chairs by the highway, stopping buses to check tax receipts of the passengers to determine if any owed taxes. At nightfall they left the tables and chairs outside ready for the next day. Sure enough, the furniture was stolen, and the officials were seen sitting in the grass by the roadside the following day, notebooks and pencils in hand.

Theft or negligence never seemed to be anybody's fault. When something was missing, stolen or broken, it was "*Shauri ya Mungu,*" the will of God. This covered everything from being given a scholarship to being caught in a crime.

With the rain, the locusts returned. They were huge, about two inches long with a wingspan of four inches. They would fly blindly against the walls outside the classrooms, losing wings or legs in the process. When the locusts disappeared, crickets came. Students were assigned to catch the survivors of the evil-smelling powder the grounds crew spread around. One day, students caught fifty-one in Miss Shrubsole's office.

The rains brought cold weather, for June was the beginning of winter in Kenya. When I went out to observe, I often wore a wool skirt and sweater and my rain boots. My students, and their pupils, would be shivering in short-sleeved cotton clothing, in rooms without doors or window glass.

Cold rain swept in, but their lessons continued.

Political discussions went on in London, and two political parties formed, Kenya African National Union (KANU) and Kenya African Democratic Union (KADU). Rallies sometimes ended with heckling and riots, and eighteen people were attacked in their homes over a six-month period.

A rash of strikes hit Kenya. In May 1962 African government employees walked out, leaving hospitals, fire departments, and police forces to be manned by volunteers—mostly Europeans. Government paperwork was neglected, and streets were left uncleaned. In June, printing and dock workers walked out, followed the next week by Nairobi bank employees. Next, 72,000 coffee workers struck, leaving the coffee beans to rot, followed by a strike of mechanics and motor company workers. Sometimes the strike was for higher wages, but other times it was for something trivial, such as support for a worker fired for sleeping on the job.

I had my own mini-strike. One afternoon when I entered an English class, the student voices greeting me had a sullen tone. They were to read a play aloud that afternoon, both for the literature and for practice in spoken English. I passed out play booklets and asked, "Who wants to read the first part?" No hands went up. I went down the list of parts, and had no volunteers.

"Right," I said. "We'll do written work." I wrote on the chalkboard some questions from the previous day's work.

The students worked through the questions, turned in papers and sat silently with crossed arms. Again I got out the play books and started asking for volunteers to read aloud. No one. I went down the list, then closed the book, went to the board and started writing up another assignment that would require even longer, more thoughtful answers.

At that point, one girl who'd had enough of writing raised her hand and said, "Please, Miss, I will read a part."

That broke the strike. Another offered, then another. We read the play. When we finished, I asked why they'd acted as they had.

"It was not you, Miss Hines," their spokeswoman said. "We were angry at another lecturer."

"That isn't the way to handle things," I said. "From now on, take up your grievance with the person concerned, and don't ever try anything like this with me again."

They grinned sheepishly and waited to be dismissed.

I was feeling more competent about grading my students, and more able to tell them how to improve. Some were very good teachers and needed little help from me. Others were mediocre, but conscientious. A third group made so many mistakes I hardly knew where to start with suggestions for improvement. They'd roll their eyes, shake their fingers at the students, mispronounce words or work out a math problem incorrectly on the chalkboard. Still, they wanted to teach, Africa needed teachers, and it was my job to help whip them into shape.

Apparently I was doing a better job than I realized. I received a letter from the director of Agency for International Development in Nairobi asking me to come and see him during the next few weeks. The first time I went he was in Dar es Salaam, the second time in Kampala. On the third try I found him in.

After the usual preliminaries he said, "We've had good reports of your work."

When I said "Thank you," he went on, "AID is planning a million-dollar girls' school in Tororo, Uganda, to be ready in early 1964. It will be secondary plus the first two years college. We'd like you to be headmistress."

"I'm surprised and pleased," I said, an understatement, "but I don't think I'm temperamentally suited to be a headmistress. I like teaching, not administrative work."

"Think about it," he said.

I said I would, and then added that I was interested in South America after I left Africa.

He said AID was spending a lot in Latin America and he'd spent two years in Guatemala. "At your age and with your qualifications, you can get a job almost anywhere in the world that you wish," he said. "If you're still interested in South America at the end of your tour here, I'll write a letter to the authorities in Washington recommending you, but it would be a shame to waste the expertise you've built up here, all you've learned about the country."

I left his office stunned. It was hard to make a decision for two years in the future. Anything could happen. Independence would happen. And what about my personal life? I couldn't picture Rico as the husband of a headmistress, living on campus, away from his own job. I didn't even consult him about it.

It was gratifying to know that I was considered well qualified for international jobs, but I knew deep down that I'd be leaving Kenya in 1963. I might come back, or I might try teaching in Texas, as the Olivers were urging me to do, but I had to go home first and touch base before I could make a decision about the rest of my life.

I needed to complete my master's degree too. I finished my thesis, retyped it and mailed it to Chapel Hill, with a cover letter saying I expected to be in the States for Christmas break in January 1963 and would like to take my oral exam then. I wrote my parents that I might bring Rico to meet them.

The college had a long weekend holiday at half-term, and mine was especially full. On Saturday afternoon I attended a cocktail party at the AID director's penthouse apartment. The main guests were officials of Columbia University who were involved with our TEA project, and dignitaries from the Kenya Ministry of Education.

The next day Rico and I drove to Amboseli National Park, in the desert area of southern Kenya, for a Ker & Downey safari, just like Hemingway and Hollywood. We were the only Kenya residents on the safari; the others were a flight crew of Lufthansa, which had recently begun air service from Germany to Nairobi.

We slept in tents that could be zipped open and closed from inside or out. At the back of each tent a separate zipped section held a canvas bathtub. Clutching my towel around me, I signaled that I wanted a bath. Stewards brought tins of hot and cold water and mixed it to my satisfaction, then went away while I sank into the tub and washed away road grime. It had been so dusty driving into Amboseli that I felt grit between my teeth.

When I finished and dressed, I unzipped the back flap so the stewards could empty the tub and turn it upside down outside to dry.

About four p.m. we went out animal-watching in a Land Rover with a hatch top, and saw animals galore: five lions asleep in a great tawny heap under an acacia tree, two elephants, a rhino, and a hyena. The trees shook from the scampering of little monkeys, and thirty baboons came right up to the camp to eat fruit peels and cornhusks.

After the game drive, Rico and I sat in front of my tent sipping gin and lime, relaxed and easy with each other, watching the star of the show, Kilimanjaro. The mountain disappears in a haze at midday, but in late afternoon it is spectacular. Its name means 'little hill of snow,' and from the safari camp it sparkled, like a big purple cake with white icing dripping down the sides. Sunset was the magical time of day. Toward the west the sun went down as a huge red ball, and smoke rose from the fragrant cooking fires. In the other direction Kilimanjaro's snow turned pink from the reflected sunset.

After dinner we had coffee and brandy and sat talking until I realized how sleepy I was. I hadn't done anything strenuous; I was just completely relaxed for the first time in months. I doused my kerosene lantern, slid under the mosquito net onto my canvas cot, pulled the blanket over me and went to sleep.

The steward awoke us at six with hot coffee and we piled into Land Rovers for morning game viewing. It was so cold my teeth chattered, and the cook was frying a huge pan of bacon over hot coals, a tantalizing smell. I would gladly have stayed in camp and eaten breakfast right then, but Rico said, "Come on, cara. We came to see animals." So I went, and I was glad.

We drove slowly toward a huge, long-tusked elephant pulling down an acacia tree for breakfast. He stuffed it into his mouth with his trunk, chewed a bit, then put his trunk back into his mouth, as though he were picking his teeth.

The game guide knew just where to take us. We saw a rhino family, herds of graceful giraffe, fields of wildebeest, zebras and gazelles, and a cheetah with two playful cubs. And Kilimanjaro showed its head above the clouds.

Back at camp, we ate breakfast at ten: strong, hot coffee in tin cups;

fried bacon and eggs; and thick bread toasted almost black over the coals. Never had food tasted so good!

Ostriches congregated at the camp entrance, waiting to be fed bananas and photographed. These beautiful, grabby birds loomed taller than a person, and would peck at anything edible or shiny. One clamped down on my finger when I held out a banana, and another pecked at Rico's watch.

Outside the park on the way home, we passed three Masai, and slowed to keep from dusting them. The two young warriors carried spears and wore the traditional rusty red clothing and beaded necklaces. Their earlobes were stretched almost to shoulder level and hung with beads. The woman had a baby strapped on her back. We photographed all three and gave them each a shilling.

Farther on, another group weren't so friendly. When we stopped for their cattle, they surrounded the car, shouting and trying to get in, and demanded the radio.

We managed to pass through the mass of cattle, and finally out on the main road we stopped at the Namanga Hotel for coffee. The hotel had a stone floor and big fireplace, and poles held up the thatched roof. Poinsettias and palms grew around the doorway, and cages of parakeets and canaries chirped away inside.

As we left, a voice said, "Emilee!" There was Kay Hinklin, my roommate from New York, the friend who'd given me Surgit. She was driving alone back to her school in Moshi from a 700-mile trip to Kampala. From Kampala she'd visited a friend at Bukoba, another two hundred miles away, where she'd gotten stranded by high water and a ferry strike. Kay was clearly the most adventurous of our group.

It was July 4, Independence Day back in America, a year since I'd stood watching fireworks in New York. Nobody celebrated in Kenya. After all, it was the British we'd won independence from. Kenya would soon have its turn.

Chapter 16: To Europe and Back

My first year in Africa had passed, and at the end of term I was going to Europe.

I wrote four articles for my college alumni magazine, studied Russian and Italian for my trip, made final plans with my travel agent, kept up with school, and got permission of the Kenya government to leave the country.

The Olivers were leaving for America. Two days before their departure, a group came from Ngelani with a basket of eggs and two live chickens, their way of thanking Chad for giving them free rides in his Land Rover and an occasional beer.

The Olivers and I flew Alitalia from Nairobi at one a.m. They had a minor accident with Ray's car within a few miles of Nairobi, and we'd all spent the evening eating and drinking too much. Kim fell asleep almost as soon as we boarded, and Chad, who hated and feared flying, was almost catatonic. The plane was hot, and Beje and I stayed awake, talking. As the announcements came over the intercom in English, I felt grateful to the British who'd taught people all over the world to speak English, and grateful that the Americans had begun commercial aviation ahead of everybody else. I could fly anywhere and understand what was said.

At least, I could until we got to Rome. On the airport bus into the city, the conductor took our entire tickets, including the portion we needed to return to the airport the following day. It took me several minutes to work out what to say, but by the time he finished his round and started back to the front of the bus, I knew how to explain the situation in Italian. When I said, "Abbiamo bisogno per i biglietti per domani," he smiled, said, "Ahh!" and gave us back the return tickets.

"See," Beje said. "Those nights studying Italian with Rico are paying off."

We slept all morning, then had an elegant Italian lunch and a whirlwind afternoon and night seeing Rome. We hired a carriage and rode among the spotlighted ruins, past the Vatican, the Fountain of Trevi, the Spanish Steps.

The Olivers' flight to Texas by way of Spain was later than mine to London, and they were still asleep the next morning when I left. In London I joined a tour that crossed the Channel and headed east by coach across Belgium, West Germany, East Germany, and Poland. I was doing this backward. Most people see England and France first, not Africa or Eastern European countries.

Belgium was a series of flat, neat fields and ornate guildhalls in ancient cities. Germany, and especially Berlin, still showed damage from World War II, some of it left intentionally as a reminder. In the divided city we took the tortuous journey through Checkpoint Charlie into East Berlin, gray and depressing. In Berlin the huge black headline, "Die Monroe est Tot!" told us Marilyn was gone.

European history I'd studied suddenly made sense when I saw how flat and utterly defenseless Poland was. No wonder it had been regularly invaded and partitioned by stronger powers. Poland was especially interesting to me, as I was writing my master's thesis on the establishment of the Polish

Government at the Yalta Conference.

We saw much of Poland in darkness, when long waits at border crossings ruined our scheduled arrival time at hotels. We ate greasy roast goose and boiled potatoes, and I missed Kenya's curry and wonderful fruits.

Finally we crossed the border at Brest-Litovsk and were in the Soviet Union, land of bureaucracy. We had to fill out forms to change our money into rubles, and account for it all when we left—no taking rubles out of the country. Intourist guides and border guards came onto the bus to look at our passports, which had already been looked at by other officials. I thought of my arrival in Tanga, when the Africans obligingly let me open my luggage to get my passport. What a difference!

We reached Moscow at dusk and saw on the horizon the lighted red star atop the main building of Moscow State University and another atop the Kremlin. Seeing Moscow was worth bad food, bureaucracy and rest stops spent squatting in swampy birch forests. Over the next few days we rode the famous Moscow subway, shopped at Guym's Department Store, saw Lenin's body, went inside the Kremlin and just stood, awe-struck, in Red Square. Russian history, from Peter the Great to Napoleon to Trotsky and Stalin, flooded over me, and I felt myself one of the luckiest of history students.

While we were talking in Red Square, two Africans approached and begged, "Talk to us in English. We haven't heard any English in eighteen months." They were Ghanaian students on scholarship in the Soviet Union, ostracized by the Russians because of their color, but there to be indoctrinated into Communism.

From Moscow we went to Leningrad (now St. Petersburg again), took a ship to Helsinki and eventually back to England. In London I spent an evening with Rico's sister. After a few days I flew to Paris, then to Zurich, and Athens. Zurich was pleasant and orderly. I drank hot chocolate and ate rich pastries, bought wool fabrics to sew, chocolates to send home and a kilo of cherries to eat right there.

Athens was another of those "pinch me, I'm actually here" places—Athens, where Plato and Aristotle, theater and architecture and democracy itself came from. From the window of my hotel I could see the Parthenon on a hillside, silhouetted against a clear blue sky. And when I looked down, I realized how close to death I had unknowingly come. I'd checked in late and never bothered to find out what lay outside my window. In the morning I opened the curtains and saw a great gaping hole just beyond a wooden crosspiece. No glass, no bars or balcony rail. One careless step and I could have plunged three stories down into an excavation.

The next day I shopped and signed up for an afternoon tour and a nighttime tour, which would end just in time for my two a.m. flight to Nairobi. On the tour were two pleasant Iranians on their way home after study in America. They urged me to visit Iran and we exchanged addresses. After Greek food, dancing, and a few glasses of ouzo, it was time to fly home to Kenya.

When I came down the steps of the plane at Embakazi Airport, I looked up at the second level, where visitors gathered, and saw Rico, waving a white placard in one hand and pink flowers in the other. I waved back and started running.

He caught me in his arms and I saw that the placard said "Welcome Home." Kenya felt like home. The flowers were pink roses.

"Thank you for the roses," I said, burying my face in their fragrance.

"They are from your own garden. I have been going there to be where you used to be, and to see that your Muyia took good care of things. I have missed you, cara."

"I missed you too, Rico. I wish you had been with me."

"Why didn't you write to me more?"

"I did. I sent you three letters and two cards."

"I only got two letters and one card, and you were gone a month. Were you too busy with your Russian lovers to write to me?"

"I didn't have any Russian lovers. How can you think that?" I demanded, furious at his accusation.

"At the club they said—"

"The people at the club like to taunt you!" I could just imagine their sneers and insinuations. "And why would I want a Russian when I have you?"

That mollified him, but it set a pattern. He'd accuse me of something, I'd defend myself and try to appease him, and we'd make up.

After a week of duty at the college, I went off to the coast—not with Ray as we'd planned three times, but with Rico. He'd borrowed a friend's house at Kilifi complete with a servant, and purchased food to take along. He'd even brought a little radio, a welcome home gift for me.

While we waited for the ferry to Kilifi, Rico bought fresh coconuts from an Arab, who slashed off the tops with a panga so we could drink the sweet juice. When the ferry docked with a rusty shudder, an African got off, said he was our servant, and crammed himself into the rear of the Karmann Ghia for the return trip.

The house was two miles out from the village, shielded from its neighbors on three sides by frangipani, palmetto and tall grass. The fourth side faced the Indian Ocean. It was an old house, white stone with a mustard yellow tile roof and a veranda wrapped around all four sides. When we went inside, I knew why the owners didn't mind our using it: little could be done to harm it. The doors didn't completely close. A dynamo furnished power, which we'd turn off at bedtime. Mildew had set in, and the bathtub was so rusty and gritty I decided I'd stay salty all week rather than sit in it.

"Maybe if we drag the mattresses out in the sunshine, they'll smell better. And I suppose the W.C. is separate, the way it usually is in Africa."

"Very separate," he said, and took me walking to the outdoor john. "Are you too disappointed? I wanted everything to be perfect for our holiday, and this is not. We can go to a hotel."

"Let's give it a try here. We've certainly got privacy. If we can't bear it, we'll look for a hotel."

That evening won me over. While Rico took a torch and went to check the dynamo, I sat on the veranda. The air stirred, bringing the smells of the sea: fish and salt and freshness. Except for the soft slush of waves and the swish of palm fronds, everything was still and silent, almost as if there were no noise anywhere on earth. Out across the water a luminescence appeared and grew. Then the edge of the moon showed above the water. I didn't hear Rico come back, but I felt his hands on my shoulders. He stood thus, silent, until the whole shape of the moon cleared the water and shone round and silvery.

"It is a fairyland, is it not, cara?"

"My life is a fairyland."

We spent five easy days, not arguing but walking on the beach, snorkeling, swimming and sunning. The closest house was half a mile away, around a curve of beach from us. I even suntanned topless, as Rico said Italian women did. He was breaking down my inhibitions.

Back in Machakos the campus seemed empty without the Olivers. I missed having Beje or Kim come to visit, but their leaving pushed me into getting to know my British colleagues better.

One night in September Rico and I gave a cookout for the faculty: he brought a charcoal grill he'd made for me and fifteen pounds of steak, and I furnished salad, potatoes and a fresh coconut cake. He was charming, and they warmed to him a bit, but most still thought him a poor second to "that nice British policeman."

Our teaching schedule that term was snarled by a strike of the local teachers, which kept our students from doing their practice teaching. I scrambled to make lesson plans on material I hadn't expected to teach. I had a feeling the teachers would lose the strike. The government had the power and the money.

Ruark's *Uhuru* was published and I read it. It was an ugly picture of what might happen after independence, and I could understand why Kenya politicians condemned it. It described illegal arms, oathing ceremonies, and armies left over from Mau Mau, which was still a fresh wound on the psyches of Europeans and Africans alike. Ruark was declared *persona non grata*, forbidden ever to return to Kenya.

Had the years of British colonization brought enough education and civilization so that uhuru would go smoothly? Or would the ordinary Africans be trading a stern British master for a worse African one? I felt sorry for those ordinary Africans, but I felt a certain contempt too for their gullibility. They would not suddenly all have Europeans' houses and jobs, as they expected. The political leaders might. They already flew to America, Britain, Saudi Arabia and even Cuba, wearing western clothing, seeking loans that might never be repaid. Then they put on tribal regalia and went out among the trusting ones, telling them how much better their life would be after uhuru.

How would independence affect our students, whom I liked and respected? How would it affect me?

Chapter 17: Springtime

It was October, springtime in Kenya. Jacaranda and oleanders bloomed in profusion, and the strip of earth between the dual carriageways of the Princess Elizabeth Highway was covered with a mass of bougainvillea—cerise, red, and purple. The short rains would soon begin, and we dreaded a repeat of the previous year.

I had new neighbors in the adjoining flat, a district officer and his wife and son. I invited them for tea, and was invited back, but they were no replacement for the Olivers.

On a Saturday afternoon Rico and I went to the Royal Show. I'd missed it the year before, when I'd monitored exams, and when Surgit had been unable to come to Kenya. How my life had changed in that year!

I enjoyed wandering around the trade and agricultural exhibits and seeing the horse show, but the main feature was the kind of ceremonial displays the British do so well. In mid-afternoon, jets from the Royal Air Force flew over in intricate, thrilling formations. The grand finale was a mass band performance of the Queen's Guards in red and black, the Kings African Rifles in leopard skins and high shakos, the RAF band, and finally two Scottish regimental bands in kilts. It was stirringly patriotic, even for an American, from "God Save the Queen"—for which we all had to stand—until the final skirl of bagpipes faded away.

Rico and I were having supper with Mario and Enrica later that month when news came of the Cuban Missile Crisis. America seemed in danger, and very far away.

Good news came from home: my sister's baby had arrived, a little girl. I had a twinge of envy. If I'd stayed home and married, I might have had a child. But then I thought about what fascinating things I'd done and was still doing since I'd left America, and my envy evaporated.

In October we had two days' holiday for Uganda's independence celebrations. Instead of going to Kampala and joining the crowd, Rico and I went to Nyeri to visit Pat McGowan. It turned out to be a dreadful mistake.

Rico felt jealous and left out when Pat and I chatted about America, what everybody on the TEA project was doing, books we'd read, our plans for after TEA.

At the club after dinner, Rico and I were out on a balcony while he had a cigarette. I knew he was angry, and I tried to defuse it before he made a scene inside.

"You don't care about me," he accused. "You only wanted to come to Nyeri to see your lover, Pat."

"He's not my lover."

"You danced with him while I was playing darts, instead of watching me. I am going to spend the night with some friends, so you can be alone with your Pat."

I had danced with Pat, and Rico had not only thrown darts, but had himself been chatting with two women.

He was sitting on the balcony rail facing me. He went on and on with abusive, baseless accusations.

I shoved him over. He fell several feet into some shrubbery and got up cursing. I fled into the club and hid out in the ladies' room until I knew he'd left.

Back at Pat's house, I cried over coffee, and he patted me awkwardly on the shoulder. He dared not do anything else. Rico's accusations had ruined our lighthearted mood.

"There's a polo match here tomorrow afternoon that I want to see," Pat said. "After it's over, I'll take you back to Machakos."

The match was at the club where Prince Phillip played when he and Queen Elizabeth had visited Kenya. Pictures of the Prince playing polo, and of the two of them in the club, covered the clubhouse walls. Polo is called "the sport of kings," but in Kenya ordinary men could play it. In spite of my distress over the ruined weekend, I enjoyed the match. I found polo fast and fun to watch—far more interesting than cricket, rugby, squash or soccer.

When we got back to Pat's house, Rico was waiting. "Get your case," he said. "If we leave now, we can get to Kampala tonight to see the end of the uhuru celebration."

I thanked Pat, apologized again and when he worried about my going with Rico, I said, "I'll be all right. He won't hurt me. And this saves you a trip." Knowing Rico was watching and waiting, I didn't hug Pat goodbye, but went to the car.

Rico acted as if nothing had happened, but after a few miles he said, "I don't want to go to Kampala. Let's head back to Machakos."

At supper that night, he said, "Never have I loved you so much as when you pushed me over. If you had not cared about me, you would have walked away after I said such stupid things, but you got angry. So I know you love me."

I was still considering flying home for Christmas, but Rico wouldn't be going along. Despite his continued talk about our getting married, I was having second thoughts. I couldn't handle his jealousy.

I swung back and forth on going home for the holidays. Airfare to the States and back cost $1300, money I could better spend in Iran and the Far East on my way home in 1963. And going home for a visit meant another tax hassle.

Finally I decided not to go, as homesick as I was. I had spent one Christmas in Kenya, and I could manage another, though I knew it would be different in 1962. The Olivers were gone, Ray was in England on leave, and all my TEA colleagues had their own schools and homes.

When I decided to stay, Rico cancelled his plans to go home as well. He'd stay in Kenya with me for Christmas.

I bought gifts to send home, in addition to things I'd already bought but hadn't shipped: A large zebra-skin drum for my sister and her husband, a bow and arrows for my brother, a woven-reed cradle for baby Elizabeth, and lion skin bedroom slippers lined in sheepskin for my father. Rico made sturdy shipping boxes and I took it all into Nairobi, where I got the bad news: the drum was too heavy, the cradle too big and the bow and arrows too long. I sent the bedroom slippers and brought everything else back to my flat. They'd had tea from East Africa the previous Christmas, not just one case, but two. I'd sent one from Nairobi that Bilbander had brought and he'd sent another from the tea plantation.

The teachers' strike was settled—in favor of the government, as I'd expected.

This was good news for us, at least. Teaching practice could be completed and our students certified at the end of term. But it was hectic trying to get in the required number of lessons in a shorter time. One week I observed twenty-one lessons and taught nine.

The first week in November I had duty for four days, including High Table, a British tradition. Miss Shrubsole, a group of students and I ate at a separate table so the students could practice making pleasant conversation while dining. She was good at asking questions that the girls had to answer with more than a Yes or No. I tried to go along with her lead, but I was relieved when it was all over, and especially glad that I didn't have to eat student food regularly. It was as bland as what we'd had at Makerere.

Two of the girls whose practice teaching I was supervising were verging on failure, and had to be observed by examiners from the Ministry of Education. They both passed. Another student we thought should fail— several of the lecturers considered her insane—demonstrated a good science lesson on the castration of goats, complete with sharp tools and a terrified, live goat. She didn't actually cut. The examiner stopped her at the crucial moment, but he was so impressed with her audacity and use of visual aids that he passed her.

One of our students who was student teaching in Nairobi ran away from the school and refused to teach. Her adviser went to the girl's home, but her mother denied she was there. The adviser returned, very worried, to determine where the student might have gone. Again she met denial, but a four-year old sister said, "She's hiding in the toilet." Sure enough, she was. She failed her teaching practice, which was sad, since she'd put in two years' study at the college. However, if she couldn't face practice teaching, she could never handle the real thing.

The college lecturers said of these disturbed girls, "It's only a temporary derangement, brought on by stress. They'll get over it." Maybe. One former Machakos student was in prison for murdering a child. Still, stress, derangement and murder were not limited to Africa. The same thing could happen anywhere.

Rico took me to Nairobi to a reception for the opening of the Institute of International Education. Gordon Hagberg, the man who'd interviewed me for TEA in Chapel Hill, was in charge. Rico left me at the door and said he'd have coffee at the shop next door and wait for me there. After about an hour I turned to go, and there stood Rico, about a yard away from me, holding a sherry glass and talking to another guest.

"A British gentleman saw me leaving for the coffee shop and said to come and have some sherry," he said, downing the last bit. "So I did, four of them." I laughed, and thought maybe he could have coped with being a headmistress's husband after all, but not mine. Anyway, I'd turned down the job.

On the way back to Machakos, we passed a herd of twenty-four giraffe close to the road. The tall, gentle animals were always my favorite, symbolizing Africa untouched. They moved gracefully, like a field of wheat nodding to a breeze, and I longed to photograph them, but I didn't have my camera along. I'd about quit taking photos, and Rico had some of my best of the two of us at the coast, to have prints of his own made.

One November day I opened my mother's letter and read, "What are you planning for Thanksgiving? A big dinner?" A quick glance at the calendar told me that day was indeed Thanksgiving Day. I was planning nothing, except making a sandwich and teaching my afternoon classes.

A great wave of nostalgia washed over me. If wishes had wings, I'd have been home that afternoon, walking in the woods, scuffing my feet in fallen leaves, helping my mother with the cooking and most of all, being with my family.

I couldn't be home, but I decided I'd tell my students about a typical American Thanksgiving. They'd gotten over their initial shyness and sometimes asked me questions about America.

I described colored leaves and snow, but leaves were always green in Kenya, and most of them would never see snow. I moved on to the beginning of the story as most Americans tell it. "The first Thanksgiving was celebrated because the colonists were grateful to God for having brought them safely across the seas to America and for keeping them alive for a year."

They knew about colonists. It was a touchy subject to them, that year before independence. One girl raised her hand. "Please, Miss, do you mean colonists like the British?"

I smiled at that. "Yes, our colonists were British too, just like yours."

The girls frowned slightly. Another raised her hand and said doubtfully, "Then perhaps the colonists here should have a Thanksgiving Day too."

There was a titter from the class and the first girl said, "The British have been here nearly a hundred years. They should be *very* grateful."

Even I had to laugh at that. I decided I'd better get on to some other aspects of Thanksgiving. I'd never really thought how it might appear from the Indians' viewpoint, but always from the settlers'. "The colonists were grateful for a good harvest."

Again there were puzzled looks. "But why did they celebrate in November?"

They wouldn't in Africa, I realized. November was not harvest but time to plant before the rains, and some crops, like bananas and pineapples, are harvested year round.

"The main idea is being grateful," I concluded, almost sorry I'd brought up Thanksgiving. "Do you have something to be grateful for?"

There was long silence while they considered. Then Mary volunteered, "I am grateful the United Nations brought maize and milk last year so my people did not starve."

Helen raised her hand. "Miss, I am glad for the chance to be a teacher so I won't have to work as my mother does. I am glad to get an education, so I shall earn a good salary. I shall never have to see my children go hungry."

I had that to be grateful for too, I reminded myself. I had an education; I received an adequate salary; and I had never had to go hungry or to work as African women did. Those students put my situation in perspective. So what if I was homesick? I had chosen to come to Africa, and I could stay to the end of my contract. My family was seven thousand miles away, but I had a good situation in Kenya.

My neighbors in the adjoining flat moved out, into an old house in town. The floors varied as much as four inches from one side to another, and in some places the wall had separated from the floor. The house had six outside entrances and about ten acres of lawn and garden.

Even after more than a year, there were still nearby attractions in Kenya I hadn't seen. In late November, Rico and I went to Hunter's Lodge, owned by John Hunter, a formerly famous 'white hunter,' author of books about Kenya. His son operated the lodge, an oasis in the desert between Machakos and the coast. We sat out on the lawn at sunset, sipping drinks and enjoying the view of Kilimanjaro. It was peaceful and lovely. Or so I thought until I had twenty mosquito bites on my ankles.

The next day we went into Tsavo Park and had lunch at Kilaguni Lodge. Down the hill from the veranda, all kinds of animals came to bathe and play in a waterhole. I liked the frisky warthogs, who trotted along with tails straight up in the air. Later, driving around in the park, we laughed at a flock of monkeys so tame and greedy that they snatched bananas from our hands and climbed all over the car. I photographed a mother monkey cradling her baby in her arms in a loving, human gesture.

We were almost back to Machakos when we saw four ostriches and a field of impala. Kenya was still enchanting. And Rico? When he was in a good mood, being around him was wonderful. But like the girl in the nursery rhyme, 'when he was bad, he was horrid.'

Chapter 18: Christmas II

December came again, and with it a lot of changes.

As Head of the Education Department, I was responsible for collecting and inventorying textbooks. I counted and stacked nearly ten thousand books, and moved from the shelves and discarded a thousand that had not been used in the four years of the college's existence. Former Heads had dutifully counted them, checked them off and reshelved them. Not me. Making the next person's job easier would be one of my contributions to the college.

I got Miss Shrubsole's permission to give the unwanted books to the students, and they happily carted them off home. I wondered where the books would go and who would read them before they finally fell apart.

December 1 was Parents Day, with the annual dance in the evening. Only a year before I had written the fateful letter to Rico, inviting him to be my escort to the dance. This time, I decided to go alone, strictly as a chaperone.

On December second, the students presented the annual Christmas pageant, with interesting touches. The student who'd demonstrated castrating the goat played an attractive Mary, plumped out with pillows to look very pregnant. The innkeeper was wearing a doctor's white gown and surgical mask, ready to deliver the Baby Jesus, and Joseph had to help the shepherds corner and control an errant goat. The richly costumed Magi and the familiar carols at least gave no surprises.

On Monday afternoon we had tea for the graduating students, and on Wednesday, after the students had gone, a tea for the workmen and their families. Miss Shrubsole announced in morning faculty meeting, "Each man will be allowed to bring to the tea one wife and three children." Some men had multiple wives and many children, and without a restriction on numbers, a party could soon get too large to be manageable. For both occasions I was asked to make egg salad sandwiches and a sweet.

End of term that year meant the end of Miss Shrubsole's tenure. She'd set Machakos Teacher Training College on the right track as its first principal and was returning to England to head up another college there. Her farewell party was an elegant, catered affair.

My parents sent a Christmas gift check that I returned to be deposited at home. It was too difficult to take money out of the country for me to deliberately bring more in. I'd passed my Swahili exam and gotten a $10 monthly raise, and when I checked my bank account I realized I'd have enough to pay my departure taxes and plane fare around the world eastward home in August, so I went on a spending spree.

I wasn't having guests for Christmas or cooking a big dinner, but I bought gifts for faculty friends and gave Muyia money and food. I knitted a blue sweater for Rico.

Then I bought clothes. The garments I'd brought from the States were threadbare, and were mostly casual. I needed dressy clothes for social events coming up. In Nairobi I bought red chiffon and taffeta to make a short evening dress for the Press Ball, silver shoes, new underwear and slacks, and fabric for three other dresses. I spent hours at the sewing machine and soon put all my new clothes to use.

Rico and I attended the charity gala film performance of "West Side Story." Everybody dressed to the nines. The Governor, Sir Patrick Renison, and Lady Renison attended, along with the mayor of Nairobi and his wife, Tom Mboya and his wife, and hundreds more I didn't recognize.

The following Wednesday we went to the Topaz Grill for lobster thermidor and champagne and dancing to an Italian orchestra. Around midnight we left and strolled along Nairobi's main streets looking in shop windows for Christmas decorations, something I'd always enjoyed doing in the States. I remembered elaborate windows with Santas, Christmas trees, ribbons and wreaths. What a disappointment! Since most of the shopkeepers were Asian non-Christians, the decorations mainly consisted of sprinkling artificial snow on whatever was already in the window.

The Press Ball was also a charity benefit, limited to 600 tickets at $5.00 each, buffet supper included. And six hundred was all the Nairobi Charter Hall could hold, especially when we were all dancing to the music of the Staffordshire Regimental Band.

Behind the band hung a huge Kenya coat of arms, its proud lion beaming down on us. When we entered, the band was tootling a highland fling, complete with kilted dancers skipping around with swords. Occasionally a Scot would shriek some clannish yell. Only in Nairobi!

My silver shoes got a real workout, as dancing went from 8:30 to 11:00 and again from midnight to three a.m. Rico and I were happiest when we were dancing together.

The buffet supper must have been wonderful. By the time we got to the tables, it looked as if vultures had been at work. Huge baked fish had only head and tail remaining, and baked capons were reduced to bones. Three whole roasted pigs were reminiscent of Victorian feasts.

The next day when Rico came for my party, he brought a mass of food and drink: two bottles of red wine, two of champagne, one brandy, one whiskey, South African pears and apples, oranges, tiny finger bananas, nuts, a tin of cookies, a cantaloupe, three kinds of cheese, olives, vegetables, prosciutto, lychee fruit, Italian Christmas bread and two bouquets of flowers.

"All this for me?" I asked, astounded.

"No, I plan to stick around and enjoy a good bit of this myself," he said with a grin.

Our guests arrived, ate and drank, and stayed. By the time everybody left, it was dark and too late to attend the Christmas carol service at church. After Rico left I sat listening to familiar carols on the radio, broadcast on BBC from Australia.

From such a wonderful Christmassy Saturday and Sunday, I awoke on Christmas Eve nauseated and aching all over with what I took to be flu. I spent most of the day in bed, but Rico took me to the club to decorate in the afternoon. We went back again late, and found four angry people eating bacon and eggs I'd ordered as part of my job as House Member.

"The Africans don't know how cook a decent supper," one complained. "You're supposed to be here to supervise."

"We had to cook our own bacon and eggs, and the bacon's bloody poor quality," another said. Somehow, though, the four of them had consumed two and a half pounds of bacon.

When I said I had flu, one said, "That's a good act."

I lost my temper and screamed that if they had a life, they'd be home or at church, not at the club complaining about bacon. Rico demanded to fight them for hurting my feelings. I went into the kitchen, dismissed the Africans for the night and hustled Rico out. The four revelers could continue drinking and close up. I remembered the camaraderie and fun of the previous Christmas, and wanted to cry.

We had Christmas dinner with the friends of Rico's. She'd prepared a lavish meal, but she had a cold and the two of us were miserable together while the men stuffed themselves.

At least Rico's sweater was a success. "No one has ever made a sweater for me before," he said, running his hands proudly over the surface of the sweater. Christmas was the hottest time of year, so I didn't expect him to wear it for several months, but he pulled it on anyway, to show me it fitted.

That night I made a drink of hot lemonade that my mother always recommended for colds and a lot else that ailed us, and sat looking at my Christmas cards.

My parents wrote that the bedroom slippers had arrived, were warm and comfy and everybody had taken turns wearing them. They were giving away tea. The second case of tea from Bulwa Estates had arrived some months before. It was wonderful tea, everybody agreed.

I had a stack of cards, from my family, people I'd worked with at the Computation Center, Jo, and the Olivers. And there was one from Ray.

Chapter 19: Uganda Again

Rico and I discussed going to the Brackenhurst Hotel on December 26, Boxing Day, for an Olde English Feast. On the 26th I still felt miserable and said I couldn't face eating anything. "But you go ahead," I urged him.

"I only agreed to go because you wanted to. You stay in bed so you'll be well enough to go with me to Kilembe."

I did feel better two days later when he came for me early in the morning. Kilembe, in far southwest Uganda, was a part of East Africa I hadn't seen. "I want to show you the chimney I built for the mines, and introduce you to the people there," he said. "They are like family to me."

"I need to stop at the bank and cash a check," I said. "I'm low on money."

"You don't need money. I am paying for everything, to make up for your bad Christmas," he assured me, so I packed quickly and we didn't wait for the bank to open.

Uganda was as green and lush as I remembered it, the shambas close together, the roads teeming with people. After the comparative emptiness of Kenya, it felt claustrophobic.

This bunch of bananas cost only a shilling

Kampala was crowded with traffic that clogged the winding streets. Bicycles wove dangerously, almost tipping with top-heavy loads. One cycle even carried a full-sized loveseat. It careened along, mysteriously finding space, and I kept expecting to see some hapless African knocked senseless by the traveling furniture.

Motorcycles and scooters darted in and out of traffic, and great smoking buses made sudden unsignaled stops.

At my request, Rico drove up the hill to Makerere and to Namirembe Cathedral, where I'd once sat in Surgit's car and looked down on Kampala at sunset. I wanted to call Surgit, but I didn't dare. Rico was jealous enough of my TEA colleagues. I didn't want to think how he'd react to Surgit. And what would I have said: You were my friend and I'm sorry I've ignored you for over a year?

The next day, we passed typical tin-roofed houses set on steeply terraced hillsides, surrounded by fringed banana plants, maize ready for harvest; and coffee trees, bearing white blossoms, green fruits and red-skinned ripe berries all at once.

Kasese was a crossroads of the railway and the highway, with a new Standard Oil station at the junction. Off to one side stood the abandoned smelting plant and the tall brick chimney Rico had built.

"It was the best of the lot," he said, "but it was in the wrong place. The workers are all needed in the mine, so they started to send the ore to Jinja. I wish you could have seen my chimney when it was belching smoke. When I finished building it, I walked around the top."

"It makes me dizzy just to look at it," I said.

He looked at it proudly for a moment, and then drove on toward Kilembe.

The towering mountains were so close they seemed to lean over the road, and I had a momentary panic that the whole range might slide down on us.

Ankole cattle near Kilembe, Uganda

The European part of town was built on the last bit of flat land before the range of Ruwenzori mountains began, and the company town for African workers clung to the slope itself.

We located his friends, had drinks and finally went back to Kasese to the Margherita Hotel.

As we were checking in I said something that set him off. He grabbed up his bag, turned and walked out, leaving me stranded.

What was I going to do? I was 800 miles from Machakos, with only a few hundred shillings in my purse, about enough to pay for the hotel room, and no way to get home. I didn't even have my passport, only a card from the U. S. Consul asking Africans to be nice to us and to call the Consulate if we were in trouble. Like Scarlett O'Hara, I decided to think about it tomorrow. I had dinner, then went to my room, got ready for bed, and watched a powerful lightning storm race across the Ruwenzori.

Handling the problem head-on the next morning, I went to the front desk and asked to see the manager. I told him my situation. "I need to cash a check to pay for my room and find out about trains or planes going to Nairobi," I said. I'd seen some tracks, so I knew there were trains, and nearly every town in East Africa had an airstrip.

He pointed to an Asian man having breakfast. "That's the regional bank manager here to audit the books of our bank. He ought to be able to help you." He gave me a single sheet of paper with the flight schedule. A plane left in three days. The ticket to Nairobi cost four hundred shillings, about sixty dollars.

I introduced myself to the bank manager and described my dilemma. "I don't have my passport with me, but I have my checkbook. Can you call the Machakos branch of the bank? They'll tell you I have money."

"Sit down and have breakfast," he said graciously, waving to a seat across the table. "There will be no problem cashing your check. I trust you.

When I finish eating, I'll give you a lift to the bank."

As we ate, he asked me questions. Was this my first visit to Uganda? How had I happened to come to East Africa, and to Kasese? I told him about Makerere and the project, about Machakos.

"I'm going back to Kampala tomorrow morning," he said. "I can give you a lift that far, and it's much easier to get to Kenya from there."

"Thank you. May I let you know later?" I didn't want to solve my problem with Rico only to get into another sticky situation. He nodded, and I saw respect in his eyes. I wasn't a pickup, despite my situation.

As I set down my empty coffee cup, a waiter came with a note from the manager: Your friend has paid your bill and is waiting at the desk.

I took my time, and when I came out of the dining room, I saw Rico. "Are you ready to go?" he asked, as if the quarrel the evening before had never been.

"Not until I cash a check," I said. I decided on five hundred shillings, the $60 I'd need for a plane ticket, plus a cushion for extras, and when I had it in my purse, I felt more secure.

"Didn't you know I would come back for you? I can never leave you," Rico said.

"You certainly did last night."

"Rico sometimes loses his temper and does stupid things," he said. "Forgive me."

"I forgive you, but you're never going to do this to me again."

"I promise. Now, let's go see this area."

We did. We couldn't go into Kilembe mine because of blasting, but I saw the outside and got a lump of ore for a souvenir. I got to know and like his friends.

Another day in drizzling rain we saw elephants and buffalo in Queen Elizabeth National Park. We drove for two hours into the mountains in search of pygmies but were only halfway and gave up. We went instead to lunch at Mountains of the Moon Hotel overlooking their wonderful garden.

I went back to Kenya determined to buy a car, and I tried. I got a ride into Nairobi and bought a Renault that had been in storage since the previous owners left the country. It seemed to be in good shape, but as I drove toward Machakos, about eight miles out of Nairobi brown liquid gushed onto the windshield. I ran the wipers, but in another mile smoke began to pour from under the hood. I stopped to check and discovered that the dry-rotted radiator hose had burst and spewed all the water out. The engine was overheated.

I hitched a ride on a lorry back into Nairobi and arranged for the car to be towed to the dealer. One of the mechanics said he'd give me a lift—but he was only going as far as Athi River. I ended up having to ask Rico to take me to Machakos.

The next day Mario took me to the car dealer and checked out the Renault. He said it wasn't worth the $500 they were asking, so I didn't buy it. I cancelled the insurance I'd bought and paid for the towing. I was still carless. I thought about the Impala sports coup with red leather interior I'd left in the States, which my father had sold back to the dealer for $800. If only I'd had it in Kenya—even with left-hand drive!

Enrica and Mario invited us to supper one night soon afterward and Rico came for me. However, instead of going toward their house, he drove toward the club and in his overly dramatic way declared, "I'm going to shove you in before all your lovers and throw money at you like Violeta in 'La Traviata.'"

He was looking at me instead of the road, and struck a bridge abutment. The car tumbled down an embankment, onto its top and then over again. It seemed to take a long time, and I wondered fleetingly what would happen when we hit bottom.

Miraculously the rolling stopped and the car landed atop a mat of thorn trees, right side up. Rico opened his door and jumped to the ground, about four feet down, then helped me down. "Are you all right? Forgive me. I would kill myself if I had hurt you."

"I think I'm okay," I said, and I was, physically. But I was angry and shaky from our near-miss accident and from his accusations.

Both the front and rear windscreens had popped out of his car and landed unbroken. He put them in the back seat just as a swarm of African men poured down the embankment, offering to help. They were from the prison, and I wondered if John, my former houseboy, was one of them. In the darkness I couldn't tell. In minutes they had lifted and shoved the car back up onto the road.

About that time, a college lecturer drove by and stopped to offer me a ride. Rico tried to keep me from leaving, but I got in her car. Rico came to my flat later, and when she asked how the accident happened, he said he'd swerved to avoid an African on a bicycle. I didn't expose his lie.

After she left, he kept apologizing for the accident and for all he'd been accusing me of. I told him to leave. I didn't want to see him for a long time.

The next morning about nine, the office clerk came to my flat to say that my friend from Athi River had called and wanted me to call him back. I thanked him, but didn't call Rico. An hour later, the clerk was back. "Please, Miss, your friend insists that you call him. I do not like to deal with him."

I didn't either. Within half an hour, Rico raced up to my flat and stopped in a swirl of dust. "Why didn't you call me?" he demanded.

"I can't take any more of your stupid accusations."

"Inamorata, forgive me. I love you and I trust you."

Another quarrel was patched over. But for how long?

Chapter 20: Faculty Friends and Rico

On the Monday after our accident, Margaret said at morning tea, "I was on my way back from Nairobi when I met a car that I was sure was Rico's. I noticed it didn't have a windscreen. Then, as I passed it, I saw it didn't have a rear screen either. Has he had an accident?"

I told her what had happened.

"Are you going to keep on until he kills you?" she demanded. "When are you going to give him the boot and admit you just have a bad case of lust?" She gave a little Tsk of disgust and turned to other topics.

My flu flared up. At least, that's what I thought it was. Or, I considered that it might be stress. I had shooting pains in my abdomen, and diarrhea. I went to a doctor, who gave me a sedative and took specimen samples. A week later the test results showed I had dysentery. I had no idea where I'd caught it—it could have been anywhere. I had to take seven pills a day, and have blood and stool samples taken once a week. I felt awful.

Another birthday came, with a flock of cards, gifts from the Olivers and Margaret, and a letter from one of the Iranians, who again invited me to visit Iran on the way home. There was nothing from Ray. A year before he'd sent me eight dozen roses.

My dysentery subsided, but I still had to go into Nairobi regularly for tests. On one of these trips Margaret took me to dinner at the home of two wealthy women who were cousins of the Sultan of Zanzibar.

Another guest that night was Charles Njonjo, an elegant sophisticated Kikuyu, who had studied law at Lincoln's Inn and was expected to become Attorney General of Kenya after uhuru. Thoroughly European despite his ebony face, he was suave in a three-piece banker's gray suit and talked of taking Home Leave—to England, when his home was a few miles north of Nairobi.

It was a pleasant, multiracial evening.

Rico stayed away for several weeks. Then one night he came tapping at my bedroom window after I'd gone to bed. "Let me in. I have some bad news."

When I opened the door for him, he said, "There is a woman in Nairobi who tells the future, and she said you are never going to leave Kenya. You are going to die here."

I didn't believe in spiritualists, but his words sent a chill up my spine. I said, "If it's going to happen, it will. Go away."

"Shh!" he said. "What's that?"

"What's what?"

"I saw a flash, like somebody taking pictures. Someone is spying on us. I'll see who it is." He dashed out and drove away.

The next night I heard something scratching at my bedroom window and saw a moving shape silhouetted against the college lights. I screamed.

"Shh, it's just Rico," he said. "I brought you a flower." He was trying to push a rose through the burglar bars. "I am so afraid for you. The woman in Nairobi—"

"Rico, I don't want to hear any more. Please leave me alone." I didn't let him in, and the next day I wrote the Catholic priest, asking him to talk with Rico and me.

They came to my flat together on Sunday afternoon. At first Rico denied going to a spiritualist, then said, "I had to find out what the future is for us."

"What you've done is wrong, Rico, and we'll talk about that later, privately. What do you want the future to be?"

"I want to marry her."

"You've come to my house the last three evenings to tell me she is unworthy of your love, and now you say you want to marry her?"

"We can't," I said. "It's been impossible from the beginning."

"Inamorata," Rico said, "you don't love me. That's what's making me crazy, making me do stupid things."

"Rico, if she didn't love you, she'd have sent for the police instead of me. But you must end your relationship. It's destroying you both."

"Is that what you want?" Rico demanded.

"It has to be." I'd sent for the priest, knowing what his solution would be. He couldn't give us a happy ending, but he could end our relationship with some dignity.

"You mean I can't come and see her anymore?"

"Stay away until you can talk to her like a friend, the way I'd visit," the priest said.

"Can I kiss her goodbye?" Rico asked.

The priest nodded and stood. "I'll be out in the car."

His going left a hole in my life, and my faculty cohorts did their best to fill his space. In one week I went out for dinner on campus four nights in a row. The next night it was my turn to entertain my fellow lecturers. By the end of the week I was glad to have an evening alone.

On a Saturday Margaret, Olive Richardson and I dressed in silk suits, hats and gloves and sallied forth to the horse races, my first time. The weather was warm and sunny, perfect for an outing, and I got into the spirit of the day. We went around to the stalls studying the horses as if we knew what to look for, and I bet on five of the six races. In the first race my horse came in last, but in the other four, he was first. I stood and cheered and imagined big money. However, since I'd only bet that each horse would show, not win, my winnings were slim. Afterward, I took the other two to supper at The Bistro. It was satisfying to go out socially with women friends. There'd be no arguments at the end of the evening, no seduction or rejection, no tears.

Olive and Margaret at the races deciding which horses to bet on

I began making arrangements to go home in August. The American Government would pay $300 of my passage, the Kenyan Government $280, and I'd pay an additional $500 to go home the way I wanted—east, around the world. The Americans, to make sure we TEAers used a 'public carrier,' would withhold 10% of the money until we got home safely and submitted ticket stubs and receipts.

I skipped Sunday services in the dining hall, since it was in Swahili. The previous week the Salvation Army had held services, and much as I respected the very real work the Salvation Army did and does, I was turned off by their services. Our students were assigned to "give testimony," reciting sins they were fighting to overcome, like pride and greed. As Margaret said, "Their scope for sin is so limited, someone else had to write their testimonies."

Saturday duty could be almost as trying as Sunday's, especially if there were a Saturday evening film. In my early March duty, a projectionist was scheduled to show "Cinderella." The students set up the chairs and at 7:15 I went over to greet the projectionist. It only took a few seconds for me to realize the film was not "Cinderella," but "Cinderfella," an old Jerry Lewis comedy. The students laughed at all the right places and didn't seem to mind the switched film, so I slipped out and had supper.

When I went back, something didn't seem right. The end was approaching, but there was still a reel of film left. The projectionist had run reel 3 ahead of reel 2. I wondered what the girls made of the film, if anything. I thanked the projectionist and supervised the students who prepared the dining hall for Sunday breakfast.

Electricity was off sporadically all week, and twice was off all night. I'd get up to a warm refrigerator and spoiled milk. We never had an explanation for the power outages, but rumors were that Africans had cut out sections of electric lines, using the copper wire to make jewelry.

The Acting Principal flew home to be with her ill mother and we all were assigned some of the A.P.'s jobs; mine was supervising the painters who were scheduled to repaint everybody's flats inside.

About that time one of my supervisors from the TEA project came for the day to observe my teaching. He urged me to sign another two-year contract, or to come back on a one-year contract, or even to agree to another term. Another term would have made sense academically, since it would have completed the Machakos school year, but it would have meant leaving Kenya in December and traveling around the world in winter.

That wouldn't have been a bad idea, since many of the places I planned to see were tropical, but at the time I turned down all his suggestions. I was too unhappy to want to stay. I was still weak from dysentery and still taking pills. And I knew I needed to leave Kenya to get away from Rico. So many things in life are a matter of timing, and this was one of them. If the TEA supervisor had asked two months later, my answer might have been different, and so would my life.

On a Saturday in late March Rico came with a typed apology for the accusations he'd made and way he'd acted toward me. I hadn't seen him in a month.

"Will you go with me to Nairobi for dinner? I want to show you I can be nice."

I said yes, and had a delightful evening. We went to the Topaz for a steak supper and a bottle of champagne. He was on his best behavior, right to the very end. When he brought me home he walked me to the door, no farther, bent and kissed me and said, "Thank you, Miss Hines."

"I enjoyed being with you, Rico," I said truthfully.

That was all the encouragement he needed.

The next day I walked across the pasture to Morning Prayer and Communion at the local church and had lunch with Olive Richardson. In the late afternoon, while I was marking papers, Rico drove up and stayed for supper. He was wearing the blue sweater I'd knitted him for Christmas.

When he asked me out for Saturday night, I accepted.

On Saturday afternoon Margaret took some students and me to the African social club for one of a lecture series on Kenya's future. This lecture, on Kenya's constitution, was presented by a BBC newscaster, who tapped on a large easel to make his points. The problem with writing a constitution in an African language, or translating it from English, showed up clearly in his demonstration. Neither Swahili nor any of Kenya's tribal languages had words that corresponded to key terms such as 'democracy' or even 'constitution.' His easel was divided down the center, with the English version, a few brief words, on the left and a translation into Swahili, often three times as long, on the right. It took a full sentence to replace 'democracy.'

Kenya's constitution, agreed on after months of conferences punctuated by walkouts, was a 247-page document *The East African Standard* called "the most complicated constitution ever devised." It divided the country into seven regions plus Nairobi, each controlling local matters like education and agriculture. The central government, made up of two houses, would control security and taxation. The Senate had little power. It could block a bill for one session, but the House could introduce and pass it the following year. Changing the constitution was nearly impossible, requiring seventy-five per cent of the House and ninety per cent of the Senate.

Finally the speaker paused and asked for questions. An obviously well-educated but also obviously drunk African stood, said, "Ladies and Gentlemen," and launched into a fifteen minute speech of his own. He was speaking English, but he wandered so I couldn't get his point. Some of our students attending the lecture began to giggle. There was no hint of a question in the African's oration.

The chairman of the meeting finally brought his gavel down sharply in the middle of a sentence. "Thank you. I'm sure our speaker will be glad to answer your concerns."

Looking as puzzled as I felt, the speaker managed to make some sense out of the remarks and answered politely. Then he said that after a ten minute break we would continue with the second half of the program, regionalism.

"We're only half through," I groaned to Margaret. Around us I saw the audience scattering for the exits.

"People are leaving."

"We can't go," she said, knowing what I was thinking. "He's prepared his lecture and come so far. It's rude to leave him without an audience. We must stay."

So we did. Margaret introduced me to a Canadian woman who'd heard I was going home by the Far East. "Do you think we could go together?" she suggested. "Two hitchhiking is safer than one."

"I'm not hitchhiking," I said. "I'm flying. Our government is paying and doesn't want me hitchhiking."

"You've got it all arranged?" she said, sounding horrified. "That takes the spontaneity out of it. I'm planning to work my way, stopping off wherever I want, for as long as I want."

"Not me. I'll be home in five weeks, God willing," I said. But I was curious. "What kind of jobs would you get?"

"Waitressing, being an au pair or whatever I can find."

"Where are you teaching here?"

"Oh, I'm not. I came on a project to help Africans dig wells and build schools. We get room and board and $1.50 a week pocket money. We thought we'd be working along with the Africans, but they don't seem to want to work with us."

I wasn't surprised. Why would Africans work for almost no wages when Europeans from afar would come and do the work? At that moment I appreciated Columbia University and USAID more than I ever had before. Compared to her assignment, mine was one sweet deal.

During the second half of the program the speaker reiterated the problems with the Northern Frontier. I thought about when I'd gone there with Ray. The Somali inhabitants of the NFD wanted to join Somalia. Riot squads were sent in after the D. C. was attacked, and a curfew imposed. In the uneasy peace, the British consulate in Somalia and the Somali consulate in Nairobi were both closed. It didn't look good for peace and unity.

It was 5:30 before we left the African social hall. Margaret knew I had a date with Rico, and I accused her of deliberately making me late. She just laughed and added, "After all, he's been late often enough."

He wasn't that time. I'd just had a bath and was getting dressed when he arrived.

Again, he was on his best behavior. First we went to the puppet presentation of "Il Trovatore," and I didn't bother Rico for translations, but just enjoyed the music. After a buffet supper, we went to the Macumba Club.

The floorshow began with a strip tease act, always popular in Nairobi, followed by a plump blonde American playing the piano and singing. She giggled and rolled her eyes as she played and sang bawdy songs, and the audience loved it. After some jazz and rock and roll, she announced that the manager had requested "Warsaw Concerto," and she played it wonderfully. I hadn't heard classic piano since I'd left the States.

One vigorous dancer, doing the twist in a pale blue satin strapless dress, popped right out of the top of her dress. She managed to push her breast back, swished her long brown hair to one side, and kept on twisting. She attracted almost as much attention as the strip tease, but her act was over quickly.

Rico wanted us to be engaged again, but I knew it was no use. I tried to make him understand, but he left hurt and angry.

Chapter 21: Kilimanjaro, Malindi and the DEO

Rico came one afternoon and asked me to play tennis at the club. I thought he was trying to show me we could do casual, friendly things together, so I went. Another mistake.

We had just come in from tennis when the District Education Officer, came over to our table. As part of my job as Education Head at the college, I had written to ask if he could come on Wednesday to talk to our students about available teaching jobs. I hadn't heard anything from him.

"Emilee, I got your letter. I won't be able to make it next Wednesday, but I can the following week," he said, and walked away, not realizing he'd dropped a bomb.

Rico stalked to his car, and was furiously silent on the way to my flat. Once there, he said, "Are you going with him on your tour to Kilimanjaro?"

"What are you talking about?"

"The DEO. It was shameless, coming up to make a date with you when I was right beside you."

"That wasn't a date. I'd asked him to talk to my students about their teaching jobs."

I might as well not have spoken. He'd made up his mind, one hundred eighty degrees off target. "Is he a better man than me?"

"I wouldn't know. Go away. I can't take any more of your jealousy and accusations."

As he left, he grabbed the radio off the dining room table. "Let someone else buy you gifts."

I should have known that wouldn't be the end of it. A few days later Margaret told me the DEO's girlfriend was upset about all the gossip about the DEO and me.

"Apparently Rico has been telling everyone at the club that you've jilted him and are having an affair with the DEO. One story even has you two marrying when term ends in July," she said with a twinkle in her eyes. "Have you been keeping secrets from me?"

"Can anybody keep secrets in Kenya? Of course it's not true. I'd never spoken to him until that day at the club. And when do you think I've had time for an affair?"

"Gossip has it that he comes up across the pasture from the club around midnight."

"How does he manage the stile in the dark? Or does he have a torch? Can't people see the absurdity of it? I hope it all blows over before I get back from Kilimanjaro." But I was wrong about that, too.

I flew to Moshi on Good Friday. At the airport I ran across two TEA teachers from Moshi who were leaving for holidays. We TEA people were like children playing musical chairs. We wanted to visit each other on holidays, but the visitee wanted to go somewhere else.

After I checked in at Marangu Lodge I walked up the hill to Kay Hinklin's school, on the slopes of Kilimanjaro. She was leaving on holiday the next day, but invited me for lunch. On the way up, I was walking slowly, gasping for breath in the high altitude, when an African came up beside me, said "Jambo," and passed me, striding easily out of my sight in a few moments.

I was lonely at the lodge, and made an effort to talk to the other guests. People recognized me as American by my accent, and I noted that the group who invited me to join their table weren't English. Their accent was unfamiliar, so I asked where they were from. "We were born in Russia and escaped in 1917. We can't go back," one explained.

They were thrilled that I'd been to St. Petersburg the year before, and peppered me with questions about their homeland. "Is the statue of Peter the Great still facing the Neva?" "Is the Astoria Hotel still there?" Finally, one said, "Tell us all you can remember of it." I did, and I compared their longing for their mother country to mine. Their eyes took on a faraway, misty look when I described Russia. If I stayed on in Kenya, in 45 years would I still be as homesick for America as they were for Russia?

Despite my loneliness, Marangu Lodge was beautiful, and if I got up early, I had a view of Kilimanjaro. From the lodge the mountain showed its two peaks, Kibo and Mawenzi; from the north it looked like a single mass. It was only visible early in the morning or in late afternoon. In between, clouds rose to cover both peaks.

I signed on for an early morning trip up to the first base camp. My wakeup call came at four, and soon several other guests and I were packed into a Land Rover in darkness and started upward. As it grew lighter, I could see that the road passed through a coffee plantation, and that snow was sifting down onto the coffee trees. I was glad I'd worn warm slacks, gloves and headscarf, and a thick pullover.

East African Odyssey

Me at first base camp, Kilimanjaro

When the Land Rover reached the end of the road, we got out and started climbing through the forest, stumbling over tree roots and stones in the near-darkness. Our driver went ahead, carrying a basket, and a porter brought up the rear, also carrying a basket and helping anyone who fell behind.

We came out onto a gently sloping plain. From there we looked down on the morning clouds as the sun rose. Our guide spread out breakfast on the stone ledge around the shelter. I was glad I'd come to Kilimanjaro, and I regretted I'd never climbed to the peak, as Margaret had done.

On Easter Monday I flew back to Nairobi and Margaret met me at The Thorn Tree with mail from the States.

After a few days back at Machakos, I flew to Malindi with Olive and Mary, two nurses. On the way we had a view from the air of Kilimanjaro for half an hour. I had begun to note things I'd miss when I left Africa, and the sight of that mystical mountain was definitely on my list.

Malindi, an old Arab port, enchanted me, and so did the Sindbad Hotel. We ate all our meals in the courtyard, amid pots of palms and bougainvillea and hanging baskets of fuchsias. In the evening we'd eat by candlelight and colored lanterns. Always the linens were starched and the service impeccable. One memorable meal began with Lobster Thermidor, moved on to baked red snapper, steak with vegetables, chicken, ice cream and coffee. Breakfast, with Kenya coffee and fresh fruit, could take a leisurely hour.

Between eating bouts, we could walk on the beach, swim in the sea or lie on the sand and watch palm trees swaying in the breeze. Peddlers sometimes approached us, but courteously. I bought hot plate mats woven of palm fronds, and Olive bought two Zanzibari copper trays and agreed to sell me her older, smaller one when we got back to Machakos.

The whole week was blissful and restful. All I had to worry about was not getting burned, looking out for crawling things on the walls and bed, and being sure to knock my shoes upside down before I put them on. Olive absently stuck her foot into her shoe and got nipped by a scorpion. Mary had a ferret in her room, screamed hysterically, and got moved to a better room.

Back from Malindi, I faced more embarrassment. Mario drove to my flat one afternoon and said, "Emilee, you should go somewhere else tonight so Rico can't find you. He has challenged the DEO to a fight."

How stupid, and how like Rico! I groaned.

Mario went on, "I don't think he would hurt you, but he wants you to watch the fight."

"Thank you, Mario. Can you do anything to stop it?"

"May be. Who knows?"

As soon as he left, I called Kay Strain, who came for me. I spent the night at her flat at the girls' school.

Mario came again the next day to tell me that he and several others had hustled Rico into the men's locker room and locked the door, instructing the African bartenders to let him out later. "I felt sorry for them," Mario confided, "because he was very angry, and it was not their fault."

How could I go to the club again, knowing the members would be snickering anew about Rico and me? And how could I face the DEO when he came to speak to my students?

On Tuesday Margaret invited me to go into Nairobi for a film. "I'd love to," I said, "but I've got duty." "We'll get Mumina to do it," she suggested.

"Suppose something happens and I'm not here?"

"What do you think your punishment would be? Would they send you home early?" She laughed at my worry.

I had my doubts, but we left her servant waiting in my house, "on duty," picked up Marilyn, my former neighbor, and went into Nairobi.

Back in Machakos after the film, we drove toward Marilyn's house to drop her off. As we passed the DEO's house, she said, "There's our car. Turn in. They're having a party."

That was the last place in Kenya I wanted to be, but there was no escape. When Marilyn opened the car door to transfer her purchases to her husband's car, the light came on. The DEO saw us and came out.

"Hello, ladies. Marilyn, your hubby's here, half potted and pinching bottoms, but we don't have enough bottoms to go around. All three of you are welcome." I wanted to slide under the seat and hide.

He opened the car door on my side and leaned in. "Emilee, sweetheart, I hear we're having an affair. Come on in and let's get to know each other. I don't know about you, but I hate to have the name without the game."

He seemed more amused than angry, so I went in with him and Margaret and joined the party. Nobody mentioned the fight, and gradually I relaxed and danced with him and several other guests. He said he'd forced Rico to admit there was nothing to the gossip. I didn't ask how. It wasn't easy to force Rico to do anything.

Before we left, the DEO asked me for a date. I laughed and declined. "You're a brave man, but I don't want to give anybody any more reason to talk about us, just when the gossip is dying down."

And the duty? The whole time we'd been in Nairobi I'd worried that something would happen while I was gone, something that would get me in trouble for shirking my duty. I didn't know what exactly I thought would happen, but nothing did.

When we got back Mumina handed me the college keys and reported that he had given the bones to Bruno, the dog—or 'Bluno,' as he pronounced it. I didn't ask if he'd made the rounds of the campus at ten, but obviously everything was peaceful.

If I'd known how competent Mumina was, I might have hired him to pull duty for me long before. Like the time I could have gone to Kitale to see Ray.

Chapter 22: Ray and Elections

There was always a surprise waiting for me in Kenya. My final term at Machakos, the principal assigned me to teach two classes of science in addition to education and English.

Science? I had never taught it, and hadn't had a scientific thought since I'd passed Inorganic Chemistry as a college freshman. Even then, the lab instructor had gotten irritated at me for only running each test once and being satisfied with the result. I didn't have the right scientific attitude, he said.

How was I to teach someone else how to teach science, when I didn't know myself? But, like a lot of other things I'd tackled, I told myself I could do it if I just set my mind to it. I read the first few chapters of the textbook and began to make lesson plans.

I could handle anything at that point, I thought. I had less than a hundred days left in East Africa, and Ray was back in Kenya from England.

I'd written him that I was no longer engaged to Rico and that I'd like to see him again if his pride would allow. He'd responded, "Your letter brought mixed feelings. When I last saw you, you seemed happy with Rico, but being a natural male, I'm glad to see my victor fall. Your ideas on pride don't quite conform to mine, but we can discuss that sometime after I return." He closed with his flight number and arrival time, but I didn't have a way to get to Nairobi and out to Embakazi, so I didn't meet his plane.

All day long, I kept expecting him to call or drive out to see me. But he didn't.

About nine, when I'd given up hope of his coming, a car drove up, but it was Rico. "I passed my tests and I'm getting a promotion," he announced. "What do you think of that?"

"That's wonderful, Rico. You deserve it. You've worked hard."

"You helped me, and I did it for you. I have been going to a psychiatrist too. Even my *mpishi* is glad about that. When I smashed the radio, my mpishi almost cried. He said I could have given it to him. It would take him a month's wages to buy a radio. I want to learn to control myself. Then I am coming to win you back."

"Don't count on me," I said. "I can't help remembering all the names you called me and the lies you told." He might even be lying about seeing a psychiatrist.

"I know, and I would cut off my arms if I could call back those ugly words. And I confess I destroyed the slides of us at the beach that you gave me to have copies made."

"Why? Those slides were precious to me. I'll never go to Kilifi again."

"I know it was stupid of me. Let me take you back to Kilifi so you can make some more slides."

"It wouldn't be the same."

He looked around my flat. "Once you prepared nice things for me. Now you prepare for Ray, but he didn't come today as you were expecting."

"How did you know that?"

"I just happened to be in Nairobi this morning, and I saw your British gentleman at The Thorn Tree. I told him you were waiting to see him."

I didn't know if what he said was true, but if it were, that alone would have kept Ray away.

Ray was posted to Nyeri, to teach in the Police Academy for his final month with the Kenya police. It was over 160 miles away, and I didn't have good memories of it after the weekend fiasco there with Rico at Pat's house. I didn't expect to see Ray for a good while, and maybe not at all.

The day after my encounter with the DEO at the party, Ray called. "I'm out of the police and working in Nairobi now. I'd like to bring steaks and have lunch with you on Sunday, if that's agreeable."

"Yes, it is," I said, trying to keep the nervousness out of my voice. "I'll look forward to seeing you."

"So shall I," he responded formally.

I wanted everything to be perfect. I set Muyia to extra cleaning, even washing the curtains and shaking out the rugs. On Saturday I made pecan pie and on Sunday morning I got up early, made yeast dough and put it to rise, then showered and dressed. I didn't want Ray to catch me messy and unprepared again. I wanted to make up to him for the shabby way I'd treated him, but how he reacted was out of my control.

When I heard him drive up, I ran to the bathroom for one last look in the mirror, and pulled the brush quickly through my hair.

He came in smiling, tall and handsome. He set down the steaks and flowers he'd brought, and taking my hands in his, bent to kiss me lightly on the cheek. It wasn't the joyous greeting of the year before, but I hadn't expected that.

Probably I should have thrown my arms around him and said how glad I was that he was back, but I didn't. We were in uncharted territory now, edgy about the past, uncertain of our future, if any.

"You're looking marvelous," he said.

"So are you," I returned inanely.

"Do we have time to go to the club for a drink before lunch?" he asked.

"Of course." Having a drink at the club would ease the awkwardness between us, put off our having to talk about ourselves. If only nobody told him about Rico and the DEO! I put the steaks in the fridge and decided that if the rolls fell before I got them baked, we'd eat something else. I wasn't going to spoil my time with Ray worrying about bread.

Before we left, Ray went to my bathroom and came out later to say, "I was surprised to see hair in your hairbrush. You're usually so fastidious."

Me—fastidious? Maybe this wasn't going to work after all.

We had a lovely day together. He talked about his new job with an industrial loan company and said he thought he'd eventually be in charge of all the offices for East Africa.

"Then you're staying on after uhuru?"

"Yes. I've got my payout from the army and the police. I can invest that somewhere and see what happens here."

"You could buy a hotel here," I said. "One at the coast went for six thousand pounds, an Asian family that had to leave in a hurry." I'd read it in *The Standard*.

"Some politician wanted that and forced them out."

"If they took from the Asians, they can take from you."

"But I wouldn't own anything here. I'll live in a company flat and have a company car."

"Don't you worry what will happen after the elections?" Elections were scheduled for the end of the month.

"I'll take my chances. I've lived in Kenya most of my adult life, and it feels like home to me."

I backed off that topic. Before he left, we made a date for lunch on Tuesday in Nairobi.

That night Rico came again, angry. "Mario said you were at the club today with your British gentleman."

"Yes, I was." I might have expected this. Kenya was a small world, where everybody knew everybody else and no secrets were kept, and Mario was Rico's friend. Of course he would have recognized Ray and told Rico. Rico had once shown my photo to a friend in Uganda who said, "I saw her at the Kitale Hotel." I'd been there twice, on the way to the Frontier the year before, and on the way back. What were the odds of being noticed? In Kenya, very good.

"He won't forgive you for choosing me instead of him. And he'll never love you like I do."

"You have a strange way of showing it. And do you realize telling people I was having an affair with the DEO could get him and me in trouble with the Ministry of Education?"

"I go crazy thinking about anybody else being with you."

"But he wasn't with me. And I intend to go out with Ray whenever he asks me. I gave him up for you once, and now I want to make it up to him."

"I don't like it, but you should give your British gentleman some time." He acted as if he owned me, and was being gracious. He left soon after.

I was determined not to let Rico spoil my last months in Kenya. I enjoyed every moment with Ray. Twice within the next two weeks I had lunch in Nairobi with him—pleasant, relaxed lunches. Time was flying too fast for me.

The rainy season came again, but didn't affect Machakos this time. The heaviest rain fell around Lake Victoria, raising the lake level a foot and causing the evacuation of lakeshore residents. And in Nairobi pipes bringing water from the highlands into the city washed away, just as our pipes had the year before, but the residents of Nairobi coped by taking fewer baths. And sales of beer and wine skyrocketed before the repairs were made.

Kenya politics captured everybody's attention. Campaigning was in full swing, with KANU and KADU accusing each other of plotting the ruin of the country.

KANU—Kenya African National Union—was mostly Kikuyu, plus two other large tribes, the Nandi and Luo. Its leader was Jomo Kenyatta, expected to be elected President in the up-coming elections. KANU's vice president, Oginga Odinga, was given to appearing at Legco in animal skins and sandals, and to making trips to communist countries. General Secretary of the party and leader of the labor unions was Tom Mboya, a Luo, who managed to get a large loan for Kenya from Israel.

How could Israel afford loans to other countries when the United States was subsidizing their country?

One of the most vocal members of KANU, Paul Ngei, called for seizure of all the Europeans' land, to be divided among landless Africans.

KADU—Kenya African Democratic Union—included the Wakamba, who lived in the Machakos area; Masai, Kalenjin and Kipsigis. Many Europeans and Asians supported KADU, which had given them more assurances of security than had KANU, and which had made more concrete plans for uhuru.

Some tribes, like the Turkana, were not even interested in uhuru, and the Somali wanted the right to secede.

KADU's leaders were not as colorful as KANU's. Its president, Ronald Ngala, was Leader of Legco. His deputy was Masinde Muliro, Minister of Commerce.

Tom Mboya thought the parties could work together. "Mr. Ngala is no hyena waiting to devour us. He is ready to listen to our point of view as we are with him," Mboya had said in 1962, but as elections grew closer, the prospects of the groups working together dimmed, and conflicts became more open.

In two different towns both parties held simultaneous rallies and fighting erupted, broken up by police with tear gas. One hapless man had his ear cut off by a panga.

The D.C. tried to stop the meetings, but the Acting Governor said banning political rallies was an infringement on freedom. Both parties had the right to make their best case to the voters. That was democracy, he announced.

In the Machakos area there was no political trouble.

Ray was busy learning his job, but he managed to get off early on a Friday and again brought steaks out to cook. The next night we went dancing at Macumba Club. He was fun to be with, easy to dance with, and I had a magical evening. Did I love him? Could he love me again? We didn't discuss the possibility.

On Sunday we drove to Nyeri to have lunch with some of Ray's friends at the Police Academy, and I enjoyed Nyeri that day, even in the rain. Ray and his buddies joked with each other, and one related the story of his brief marriage. He'd brought the bride-to-be out to Kenya after a short acquaintance in England. "She'd never been off the tarmac," he said, using the local ad claim about a good used car to indicate his bride's chastity.

"And didn't get off it with you either," the other hooted, meaning the marriage had never been consummated.

The bridegroom, a staunch Catholic, had been trying for six years to get his marriage annulled after his bride ran off with his best man. Later, when we were discussing world news, the jilted bridegroom mentioned that the Pope was ill.

"Probably tripped over your file," Ray said, and everybody laughed. This jocular Ray I hadn't seen before.

Rico showed up unexpectedly at my flat on Saturday night. "I'm surprised to see you here on a Saturday," he remarked, obviously pleased.

He handed me a bottle of wine and I poured us each a glass. "What were you going to do with the bottle of wine if I hadn't been here?" I asked.

"Drink it all myself, most likely. You are not out with Mr. Ray. He must be out dancing with someone else."

That thought had occurred to me too, but I wouldn't let myself dwell on it. Ray had every right to date someone else as well as me. "He may be. He said he had friends from up-country visiting."

"He'll never marry you, but I would."

"Don't start that again. I can't live having to account for every moment of my day and worrying about speaking to a friend for fear you might get jealous."

"I have changed, cara, and I can change some more."

"I know, but we can't change what we are. You need to find a woman who loves you the way you are."

"But it can't be you?" he asked mournfully.

"I want to spend time with Ray and see what happens. I've got to get over you."

"Inamorata, I'll never get over you."

He set down his wineglass and stood. "I am going. I won't do anything to embarrass you with your British gentleman, but if you want me back, I will come. Will you kiss me goodbye?"

I felt the brush of his moustache a second before his lips touched mine. He kissed me gently and then pulled away from me, and with an agonized cry, he plunged outside. I heard the furious whine of the Kharmann Ghia and the spray of murram as he drove away, the sound fading into the African night.

He didn't come back.

When I awoke the next morning it was pouring rain. So much for sitting outside with Ray enjoying the garden Muyia had worked so hard on. He'd cut the grass, gotten up all the dead leaves from the geraniums and removed every weed from the garden plots, but who could tell now? I put on my raincoat and boots to get lettuce and radishes for salad.

Ray and I had planned to play tennis but the rain marked 'Paid' to that, as the British say. He arrived in shorts, carrying bags of fruit and a bouquet of red carnations and white asters. No more roses for me.

We sat around all day eating, talking and sipping wine. Being with him was like having the sun come out after a storm. We didn't talk about the future, ours or Kenya's.

Kenya's elections went on for nine days: two days for local balloting, two days for regional, then a day off; then two days each for the two chambers of the legislature (House and Senate). Because so many of Kenya's voters were illiterate, each political party had a symbol on the ballot.

The three main ones were an open hand, a closed fist, and a cockerel. Workers had to be given a half day off four times to go and vote, so work schedules were disrupted all over Kenya. Those working a long way from home had ten days off to go home for the entire elections. No one thought of absentee ballots.

Things were surprisingly peaceful during the elections, except on the Northern Frontier, where four people were killed. I was glad that Ray was out of the police, but if he hadn't been in the police at Machakos, we'd never have met.

On Wednesday I was in Nairobi with Ray when word came that KANU had won the elections. Kenyatta, now Kenya's President, declared a holiday for Saturday and Monday. "Let's go away this weekend," Ray suggested. "We can visit Nancy's farm. It'll be a good time to be out of Nairobi."

The holiday was bad news for the college. Our students were scheduled to begin their practice teaching on Monday, and now they couldn't. I worked into the night Thursday and Friday preparing them. When they all left on holiday Saturday morning, so did I. I went into Nairobi with Olive, met Ray there, and we drove up to Nancy's farm in the Kinangop, at 9,000 feet altitude.

It took forever to get clear of Nairobi. The shops, restaurants and cinemas were closed, and the streets were clogged with Africans walking, or riding bicycles, cars and lorries. Some of the lorries were loaded with people hanging on every which way, clutching baskets of chickens and live goats. Everybody we passed waved flags. Some raised fists and screamed at us, a pair of Europeans. A few stones got tossed at the car, and I kept twisting around nervously to see what would come next, but Ray took it calmly and kept driving, slowly and deliberately.

At the farm, Ray carried in the basket of food he'd brought and we went to warm ourselves by one of the immense fireplaces before sitting outside in the sunshine drinking coffee. Nancy apologized for the overgrown garden, a mass of flowers and vegetables together, but I liked it. It reminded me of my Grandma Hines's garden. Carnations, roses, sweet peas, chrysanthemum, calla lilies, larkspur and iris bloomed all at once.

The house was stuck against the hill, about halfway up. It had been built in stages, but the different-aged buildings were melded together by some leafy vines that almost obscured the dining room and kitchen windows. Along the front walk were cedars that whistled in the wind, and the whole thing smelled wonderful: a mixture of cedar and roses, and of smoke that curled from the cooking fire in the kitchen.

Some workers came up the hill, chanting in Kikuyu. Nancy translated. "They're celebrating uhuru. They say they will be masters of their own country when the Europeans leave. But they may be kind to me since I have been a fairly good Memsahib."

"Did you have any labor trouble during the elections?" Ray asked.

"No *trouble*, unless you count doing a lot of the work myself. Most of the workers claimed they lived far, far away, so I had to give them the whole ten days off."

"Are you staying on?" Ray asked her.

"Of course. This is home."

After lunch, while the other guests were taking a nap, Ray tapped on my door and asked if I'd like to walk around the farm.

As a member of the British Army sent to fight Mau Mau during the Emergency, he and his team had camped on Nancy's farm. He showed me where they'd set up a trip wire and flare on the Mau Mau supply route. "When anything came along, the place lit up like midday for a split second, and we were all lying in wait with our guns aimed along the trail. A lot of nights nothing happened, but one night we got a buck and two Mau Mau. Then a few minutes later we bagged a bread truck. We didn't know what was going on when the truck pulled up and stopped, but we grabbed the driver. He'd hijacked the truck from a Nairobi bakery and was delivering food to his comrades. A few minutes later his contact showed up. We sent them both to detention camp."

"Were you ever frightened?"

"My first night on ambush I was sweating so I didn't think I could pull the trigger, but I had to keep control for the sake of the Africans in my command."

"Did the killing bother you?"

"It did until I saw what the Mau Mau had done to a village—killed everybody there and mutilated them. Heads lopped off, bellies slit, intestines pulled out, genitals cut off and stuffed into people's mouths. After that I wanted to kill as many as it took to stop the horror." He shrugged, as if to break the spell of the memory. "I'm sorry. Let's not talk any more about the Emergency. Let's just enjoy walking."

We walked to the top of a hill with a sweeping view of the Kinangop valley and beyond to the volcanic peak of Mount Longonot. He put his arm around me and we stood in the chill air for a few minutes, he probably still recalling the past, and I wondering about the future. I could live here like this, I thought, but this is going to disappear.

When we got back to the house it was teatime that became supper. Afterward, Nancy's house servant brought hot water bottles for everybody to take to bed. I slipped mine under the three quilts I slept beneath, and fell asleep.

On Sunday we drove to The Brown Trout, a rustic wood-paneled inn with fragrant, crackling fires and lovely old furniture. I'd heard about Kenya people spending romantic weekends at The Brown Trout, and it was a good place for an assignation. We had drinks and a leisurely old-English style lunch. After coffee in the lounge by the fire, we strolled down to the trout stream.

On Monday Ray and I climbed to the crater rim of Mt. Longonot where the air was thin and cold, even in the sunshine. Ray, always thoughtful, had remembered to bring along hats to shield us from sunburn, but my neck turned an unattractive red.

After the weekend holiday, it was back to work, making up for missing a day of practice teaching. During the week I graded all my exams, taught five lessons, observed eighteen, and got into Nairobi to have a tooth filled.

I observed two days at St. Mary's, the little Catholic school near Mario and Enrica's house, and she invited me to come for lunch and use their bathroom. She and I had remained friends in spite of Rico, visiting each other and chatting comfortably.

Because St. Mary's was Catholic, it was difficult to schedule enough practice teaching for our students. All one morning the priest had confession, and I couldn't help wondering what those poor, thin children had to confess. Another day there was a Mass for the Pope.

One of my students was teaching first grade totally in English instead of Kikamba, and I found what she was doing fascinating. During the whole lesson I observed, she never said anything in Kikamba or Swahili. She gave commands in English, such as "Raise your hand," while doing so herself. The students repeated her words and mimicked her action. Then she touched her lips for silence and said again, "Raise your hand," and they did.

This is how language should be taught, I thought, by total immersion. It's the way babies learn language, being surrounded by talk and having to figure out what's what.

That weekend Ray and I visited friends of his toward the coast. They only had one guest room, so Ray camped out on the lawn in a tent. "I don't mind," he said. "It rather reminds me of police work." I wondered if he'd be happy sitting in a loan office all day, after ten years of being outdoors.

One of their neighbors was rearing a baby rhino whose mother had been killed by poachers. When he came visiting, it trotted along with him, looking as cute as a baby rhino could look. It weighed 145 pounds at three months, and was drinking gallons of milk every day, hand fed with a bottle. He liked being patted, but his hide was already so tough that patting him was like touching a cement wall. Like all baby animals, his feet looked too big and clumsy for the rest of him. He was just beginning to eat leaves, and pulled down and ate an ornamental vine from our hosts' front porch.

The following weekend Ray visited friends in the Highlands without me. On Saturday afternoon I walked across the pasture to the club to watch a rugby match. I'd never seen one, and I thought it would be a shame to leave Kenya without watching at least one match. Kay Strain was there with her date, a forestry officer. Peter, another forestry officer, offered to bring me home, so I stayed for supper and dancing. We made up a foursome, and I had a good time—without Ray or Rico, and without complications.

The next Wednesday I went into Nairobi with Olive to get my hair cut, my watch repaired, and my going-home schedule worked out.

I met Ray after work for dinner at the Pagoda. I'd come full circle, since the Pagoda was the first place we had gone on a date nearly two years before. But the circle was closing too on our relationship. He was leaving for South Africa and would be there when I left for the States.

When he came out to dinner the next night, we talked while we cooked, and I knew Rico had been right. Ray would not be marrying me. "I wish you were staying on," he said, "but I can't ask you to stay for me. Or ask you to come back. It would have to be your own decision. I don't know how I'd feel about you later."

"I wish you were coming to the States with me."

"My life is here."

I knew I wouldn't be happy living away from my family, in the Kenya of the future, and Ray would never be happy anywhere else.

We parted on good terms, but with no promises of getting together and no vows of love.

Chapter 23: Leaving

I still had a month of school left, but I was focused on going home, and on what I would do afterward.

On the second anniversary of the day I'd left home, I went into Nairobi to be interviewed for a graduate fellowship open to people who had taught overseas for two years. It turned out to be a mini-TEA reunion. Nearly half the teachers on the project were there.

Pat McGowan and another teacher came on to Machakos afterward and spent the night at my flat. They had a rugby match in Nairobi the next day. Pat and I were still buddies, and might have been something more under different circumstances. He tactfully didn't mention the dreadful night Rico and I had spent at Nyeri. He did ask at one point, "Are you still engaged to that Italian?"

"No. I'm totally unencumbered now, and I'm going home."

My travel schedule was exciting. I'd always loved traveling, and my favorite song in college had been "Faraway Places." Now I was going to see some of those 'faraway places with strange-sounding names': Cairo, Beirut, Tehran, Isfahan, Karachi, Delhi, Calcutta, Bangkok, Tokyo.

On my next trip into Nairobi, I went to the East African High Commission to arrange for my taxes to be taken out of my bonus and leave pay. I'd still have $600 to spend on the way home.

While I was in Nairobi, I had a cholera shot, required for visiting India. By the time I got back to Machakos my arm was beginning to swell and I felt a little woozy.

I planned to sleep all afternoon, but Pat and a friend showed up unexpectedly. They wanted to see the rugby match at Machakos and stay over for another on Sunday.

After the match we went to a Wine and Cheese Party at the home of some original Kenya settlers about forty miles away toward the coast. The party was a fund-raiser for the Machakos swimming pool project.

Dozens of cars littered the yard where the party was being held, and the house itself was lighted from end to end. Queasy drinkers and lovelorn couples wandered outside, and from the house came the sound of laughter and talk. I scanned the parked cars and didn't see Rico's, so I relaxed.

Doors were flung wide open and tables had been set up on the veranda that circled the house. In the lounge a log fire burned in a big fireplace, and another fire glowed in a barbecue pit outside. The back veranda was the bar, where Pat and Milt went to buy wine.

For our donation we got cheese and wine, salad, fruit, dessert and coffee. A woman sat out by the barbecue pit strumming a guitar and singing soft folk songs, while a stack of records played itself out in the main lounge, and fit and unfit attempted the limbo. It was a good party.

I was enjoying myself, standing by the fireplace with my arm on the mantel, chatting with a KBC announcer, when everything suddenly went black. The next thing I knew, Pat had caught me in his arms and was leading me outside. "Are you all right?" he asked. "I didn't think you'd had that much to drink."

"I didn't. It's the cholera shot," I said. "They warned me no alcohol for twenty-four hours, and I forgot."

"Wine is alcohol, all right," he said, easing me to a seat by the barbecue pit. The guitar player had gone inside, and we were alone. "Feeling better?"

"Yes. Can we sit out here and talk? I really don't feel up to the limbo—or anything else."

"Sure. Scout's honor, talk is all I'll do. Here, see both my hands. I won't take advantage while you're woozy. So let's talk. What are you going to do back home?"

The question we were all asking ourselves and each other. "I don't know. What about you?"

"I've got another year here. Then a doctorate in something."

"I came planning on staying two years, and it's almost over. When I planned to marry Rico, I knew it meant a lifetime away from the States, but that didn't bother me at the time. Or maybe it never sank in. Marrying him was too unrealistic. When things got bad, I prayed to get away from Kenya. Now I'm enjoying it the way I should have all along. No attachments, no involvements, just taking things as they come. Now I could consider coming back."

"So could I," he said.

A few days later I had to have another shot. A case of smallpox showed up in Machakos, so we were urged to have inoculations. I'd had one at age seven, one when I went to college, another when I went to graduate school and a fourth before leaving for Africa, but I headed down to the clinic for another round. I didn't want to be sidelined with smallpox, so close to the end of my contract. For that matter, I didn't want smallpox ever. In Machakos we got live virus, and my arm swelled, turned red and had an oozing sore that crusted over. The inoculation definitely "took."

I was paring down. I gave Margaret my Harry Belafonte albums and Enrica my Mario Lanza album. I arranged buyers for my mattress, mosquito net and refrigerator, and dispersed paperbacks and unwanted clothing. The day I took my typewriter and other sea freight into Nairobi for shipping, I got a lump in my throat. Sending the last things home was so *final*.

I was feeling pulled in two directions: homesick, but enjoying Kenya; longing to get home, but wondering if I would fit in at home or if I had changed so much that I would be a stranger in my own country.

Letters from my family pulled me homeward. A good week in Kenya made me wish I'd signed on for another tour.

My colleagues at Machakos were looking for other jobs and calculating how much their pensions would be if they went soon, or if they should take a chance on a few more years of the good life in Kenya. Mohan had been gone nearly a year. Farm families who'd been three generations in the country were bitterly selling for less than half what their land and livestock were worth, knowing that in another year or two they might not be able to sell at all, for squatters would have moved in. Every family, every teacher and administrator, every friend who left took away a small piece of the Kenya that had a special place in my heart.

In the midst of dismantling my life in Kenya, I thought a lot about what I'd accomplished, and about my relationship with my students. It had been developing slowly, subtly, almost unnoticed. I'd been very conscious of my relationships with my colleagues and with Ray and Rico, but took for granted the most important, that with my students.

I never had a discipline problem in Kenya. My students' docility, trained into them all through school, was in some ways a disadvantage. They seldom asked questions or let themselves be drawn into a discussion in class, for fear of offending someone or making a mistake that everyone could hear, and thus losing face. Their answers on exams were a repetition of what the book had said or what I had written on the board. They never took the initiative or even considered that there might be more than one way of looking at a question. The teacher's word, even wrong, was accepted.

They had been slow to trust me or to allow their feelings to show, and at first I too was cautious with them. I was conscious of the difference in race, and careful not to say anything that would offend them. They were puzzled and uncertain about American attempts at friendliness, and instead of responding to my jokes or questions the way American students would have, they would turn their faces into masks that hid all emotions.

Only in my second year had they begun to open up, to ask questions and to talk freely when they came to my flat for tea. One of my most satisfying moments came unexpectedly. In one of their reading selections there was a mention of a Freudian slip, and I explained what it was. Usually they managed to use a new word or term soon afterward in my presence, but not that one. In my last month in Kenya, I made such a slip while we were setting up chairs for an assembly program.

Immediately all chairs were still, and the class as one crowed, "Freudian slip, Miss Hines!" They were pleased that at last they had found an opportunity to use the new term, but I was even more pleased that they had felt free to joke with me.

Had I changed their lives? Perhaps by exposing them to an outsider who was not British I had made them aware of other worlds and cultures. And surely, the other lecturers and I had helped prepare them for teaching careers so they would not live and work as their mothers and grandmothers had.

One of our former students, now out teaching, wrote a thank-you note back to the faculty. After mentioning several others she was grateful to, she added, "And I want to thank Miss Hines for teaching me how to keep school records." That may have been my major contribution to East African education. Records are important.

Not wanting my replacement at the college to face the same situation I'd had—making exams on material I hadn't taught—I made out exams for the newcomer to administer, made notes on what I had taught and suggestions of work she might cover.

Whatever I had done, for good or bad, it was almost ended.

The last weekend before I left, Mary Kelly and I went to Narok to visit two other teachers and see the animals in what later became Masai Mara Game Park.

Cliff Shaw, the headmaster, was British. He said he had a member of TEA recently assigned to his school, but I didn't know him. His group arrived in Africa a year after mine. At that point I wasn't interested in meeting any new people. I was leaving. I thus missed a chance to meet Lloyd Sherman, who has since become my friend.

Things were winding down at Narok as well as the rest of Africa. Cliff was leaving at the end of term and had already sent home some of his household goods. He was short of blankets. I was glad Mary and I had brought along our coats as he'd suggested. It was so cold we slept in them.

The school was being Africanized and most European settlers had already left. Cliff and Greg were the last two members of the European club in the village. It had an impressive stock of liquor, which they were manfully trying to drink up before they left. When we went for drinks before dinner, Cliff said, "I'll treat tonight," knowing there was no charge. For the second round, Greg said, "This one's on me, old boy. I insist."

Our host had laughingly told me earlier that his houseboy ironed the table napkins according to what status he put on the guests: the more important, the fancier the napkins were folded. I looked carefully at ours, folded in a simple tulip fashion, and decided that we rated above average, but not tops. I caught Cliff's eye and remarked on how nice the napkins looked. He looked sheepish.

Greg, Mary and Cliff at Narok

Tying up loose ends before I left Kenya, I had written to Surgit several weeks before, telling him how much I appreciated his friendship in Uganda and that I was leaving July 31. I gave him my address in America. One day in late July, the Acting Principal came by my flat to say that a Surgit Toor had called and she had assumed I didn't want to talk with him and had taken the liberty of telling him I wasn't available. To my shame, I didn't call him back.

Everything had to be finished up, all the textbooks counted and shelved, records completed. My flat had to be cleaned and the electricity turned off. Everybody invited me for lunches, dinners, and drinks, offering in a few days what should have been months' worth of hospitality. Two nights before I was due to leave, the faculty had my going-away party. I'd promised myself I wouldn't get sentimental and teary-eyed, but I did. I don't remember what I said when the Assistant Principal thanked me for my service and wished me a safe journey home. I only know I couldn't say much for the lump in my throat.

I moved in with Margaret for the last two nights, so my flat could be inspected, readied for the next occupant, and locked.

The night before I left, Enrica came and asked if I'd go with her to the club for one last time. As I got in her car, I asked, "Will Rico be there?"

"Yes," she admitted. "He asked me to bring you. He said you wouldn't ride with him."

I didn't know if I could face him at the club. What embarrassing thing would he say or do? Enrica understood and said, "It will be all right. He won't cause trouble tonight. He just wants to see you."

We'd only been at the club a few minutes when he came in. I saw him across the room, and my heart lurched. Someone put on a record then, Ray Charles singing "I Can't Stop Loving You." I don't know if Rico requested it, if someone played it as a cruel joke, or if it was just a sad coincidence. He had dominated my life for a year and a half. I thought of all we had meant to each other, and all we had said and done to hurt each other, and I saw him through a shimmer of tears.

As he came toward me, everybody stopped talking and watched us, probably expecting fireworks. We had certainly provided enough in the past, but we would not that night. He stopped in front of me, held out his hand and asked quietly, "Miss Hines, may I have this dance?" just as he had the first night we met.

I moved into his arms and as I leaned against him I felt his face was as wet with tears as mine. I was crying for what had been, for what might have been, and for what I had ruined by loving him.

We moved slowly around the floor, all alone, tears pouring unchecked down both our cheeks.

"So you are really going, cara?"

"Tomorrow. Would you like to go to the airport?"

"No, I can't bear to see you fly away. I want to remember you like this, dancing in my arms, to the end of my life."

When I came out to go to the airport the next morning the stars were still shining in the dark velvet sky. In the chill, a delegation of my students, wearing their robes and nightgowns, waited to tell me goodbye.

These were the group who had been mine for five terms. In a few months they would graduate and become teachers. I recalled walking with them to their schools, discussing their teaching problems, sitting in cold, damp classrooms observing how they would shape their pupils' and their country's future. We had not become friends—the college was not set up for that—but we liked and respected each other, and that was satisfying enough.

When I'd first met them, I couldn't tell them apart, but I had come to see them as individuals, and I knew all their names and personalities. I went down the line, shaking hands with each and promising to write. The last in line, their spokeswoman, gave me a tablecloth they'd hemstitched and embroidered themselves. "We all worked on it a bit," she said. "We want you to have something to remember us by."

As if I could forget!

AFTERWORD

I had an exciting trip home in 1963, adventurous enough to make up another book, as I traveled north to Egypt and Lebanon, east to Iran, Pakistan, India, Thailand, Hong Kong, Japan and Alaska, stopping in California to visit friends from graduate school, and then crossing the continent to Virginia.

I completed my master's degree and moved to Austin, Texas, to work for the University. The Olivers welcomed me and I dated their friend Jim, but soon realized he was not right for me. Two years later, visiting my parents, I met and married Tom Cantieri, who was my loving husband until his death in 2003. Our daughter Catherine graduated from the University of Texas, and became friends with the Olivers. Beje and Kim still live there. Chad died in 1994.

The same month that I married (July 1966) Ray and Rico both married. I learned later that a large group of TEAers all married in 1966. It was a good year.

Rico returned to Italy, where he died in 1999. Ray lives in South Africa on a game ranch. In Jan 2011 I visited the ranch, Ants Nest, and enjoyed reliving Kenya days with Ray. I've kept in touch with Enrica and Mario, and visited them in Italy in 1970. In 1982 I visited Kenya and drove out to Machakos. So many houses had been built near the college that I could hardly find it.

In the late 1960s, I sent money to Muyia to buy coffee trees and a tractor, but I have lost touch with him.

Margaret Lloyd and I remained friends and traveled together many times. In 1998, Margaret and I visited Hazel Bak in Northern Ireland; Hazel died in 2004. Both Olive Richardson and Mary Kelly died of cancer.

In 2000, Margaret arranged a Machakos reunion at her home in Cheltenham, England, where I saw again Alison Shrubsole, Cecily Neville (both of whom died in 2003), M.E. Anderson, M.P. Anderson, and Gina Naldrett Poole and her husband Eric. Gina and Eric had visited us in the States and Tom and I had visited them in Canterbury. Margaret Lloyd died suddenly Jan. 24, 2005.

As decades passed, I lost touch with all the TEAers except Kay Strain. Then in 2000 Edgar Schmidt (TEA I-A) retired and began searching for TEAers. Being "found" and finding others was a wonderful gift—a part of my life that had been missing. I volunteered to gather information and photos about TEAers and put together an album for our 2001 reunion.

At the same time, I began writing *East African Odyssey*, and wanted to locate Surgit and Mohan. Surgit had last written me from Dar es Salaam in 1965, inviting me to visit. In 2001 I wrote a letter to the *East African Standard* asking if anyone knew of him. An e-mail came from his friend, reminding me that Surgit and I had spent the night at the morgue. The following day I had an e-mail from Bilbander Gill who remembered my visit to the tea plantation at Tanga and our trip to Dar. He said Mohan had died ten years before in Los Angeles and Surgit had died in 2000, back in Kampala. Bill has since disappeared.

Joan Hoffman married Jerry Schieber, also of TEA, and lives in New

York. Kay Hinklin married an Italian, Alberto Mongardi, in Moshi; their land was seized and they and their two children moved to Sudan. Following his death, Kay accepted teaching jobs in various countries and is now living Italy and directing International Schools.

Kay Strain married in Kenya. After her divorce she married Danny Borkowski and lived for several years in Cyprus, where I visited them in 2004. They have recently bought a house in Mexico.

Gene Ashby, married and divorced, taught in Pohnpei and wrote extensively about the South Pacific. He died in 2002. Pat McGowan divides his time between college teaching in South Africa and Arizona. Rufus and Doris Sanders have disappeared.

In 2003, 28 of us who had taught in East Africa in the 1960's made a trip back, visiting Makerere and schools we'd taught in, meeting with education ministers and diplomats and former students. One of my former students, Rose Mudavadi, visited with me several times during our stay in Nairobi and she and her husband, former ambassador Justus Mudavadi, took me out to lunch.

Me with Rose Mudavadi, a former student

Three TEAers joined me for a trip to Machakos. The college has four times the enrollment it had in the 1960s and many of the buildings are dilapidated, but there is hope that with the new government Kenya will spend more on education. The country has already begun to limit its growing population, which is ten times what it was when we lived there.

Machakos Teachers College is now two stories, 2003

We TEAers had our 50th anniversary in June 2011 at Columbia University, where we trained. How could 50 years pass so swiftly?

East African Odyssey

TEAers at Kenya Parliament Building, Nairobi, 2003

My two years in East Africa were exciting, inspiring, frustrating—and sad. If anything in life could be repeated, I'd relive those two years and do a few things differently. But overall, it was wonderful.

About the author

Emilee Hines graduated from Lynchburg College and has a Master's degree from UNC-Chapel Hill. She taught in Virginia and Kenya, and is the author of nine non-fiction books, three romance novels, a comedy novel, a self help book, *Til Death Do Us Part*, and more than 300 articles and short stories. She lives in the mountains of western North Carolina. Visit her web site at www.emileehines.com.

Made in the USA
Charleston, SC
25 May 2013